The conversion from the Military to a Civilian is quite difficult and there are many soldiers who were left behind to suffer on their own. It's the strength of the brotherhood that has kept them moving, one step at a time.

FROM SOLDIER TO CIVVY

It's A Journey...And I'm Not The Same Anymore
RICHARD (ERNIE) OKRAINEC

Seeing this inspired me to write about my journey, with the hope, it may help them get by.

This is just a story of how I managed to come out the other side.

So this story is for them, to let them know they are not forgotten.

Richard Ernie Okrainec
VP

**FriesenPress**

Suite 300 - 990 Fort St
Victoria, BC, V8V 3K2
Canada

www.friesenpress.com

Copyright © 2018 by Richard (Ernie) Okrainec
First Edition — 2018

All rights reserved.

No part of this publication may be reproduced in any form, or by any means, electronic or mechanical, including photocopying, recording, or any information browsing, storage, or retrieval system, without permission in writing from FriesenPress.

Special thanks to my direct family and the military family. Some photos in this book have been obtained from various military sites.

ISBN
978-1-5255-2922-1 (Hardcover)
978-1-5255-2923-8 (Paperback)
978-1-5255-2924-5 (eBook)

1. Biography & Autobiography, Military

Distributed to the trade by The Ingram Book Company

TABLE OF CONTENTS

Forward	v
Intro	vii
Prologue	xi
Chapter 1	
CFRS (Canadian Forces Recruit School) Cornwallis-Nova Scotia-Fall 1980	1
Chapter 2	
Wainwright Alberta-1981	11
Chapter 3	
CFB-Kapyong Barracks-Winnipeg, Manitoba-Summer 1981	15
Chapter 4	
Fort Reilly, Kansas And Back-1982	31
Chapter 5	
Cyprus-Winter Tour Oct 1982- Apr 1983	39
Chapter 6	
Flyover-Germany-Fall 1983	53
Chapter 7	
CFB Baden-Sollegen-West Germany-1984-88	61
Chapter 8	
Well here I come. Hello Civvyland-1989-Present	121
Chapter 9	
The Wrap-up	165
But first: The Dirty Patricia	167
Just how should I feel	169
Chapter 10	
Conclusion of it all	179

FORWARD

Robert (Clay) Rankin
Sgt.-PPCLI
Retired

Given the privilege to read the sneak preview, it was immediately obvious to me that Richard's book is meant to be read in his voice – that is to say, imagining Richard narrating it, sitting by a fire, drinking a beer. He writes like he speaks, full of the colourful jargon we all became familiar with from our time "in".

Richard (I still stumble over his proper name, having known him for almost forty-years as "Ernie"), was not an army lifer, but as with many of us, our evolution from teenager to adult under the tender ministrations of Cornwallis and Wainwright military instructors and then the seasoned NCOs (Non-Commissioned Officers) of Battalion bestowed a strong sense of loyalty and camaraderie that is sadly almost non-existent outside the bonds of Regimental brotherhood. His successful conversion to civilian life no doubt benefitted from the "soft" skills he picked up as an infantryman (lol).

I personally had the good fortune of knowing and meeting Richard's family and was invited to play on the family-based slow-pitch team for a few memorable tournaments. Our team's clumsy attempts at "moon-walking" to celebrate every out kept us in stiches and the other teams confused.

When Richard pulled the pin, I lost touch with him for several years – knowing that he was in Brandon had me feeling guilty whenever I drove past on Hwy #1 that I wasn't making more of an effort to touch base with him. Hearing he was involved in radio gave me a wry smile, since we had worked together in

Signals Platoon, and if THAT doesn't prepare you to slip right into a job at a civilian radio station, I don't know what does!

This book walks us through the trials and challenges Richard faced throughout his life and careers, during his transitions from civvy to soldier to civvy again and demonstrates the possibilities if one is determined to "endeavor to persevere".

Richard downplays his dedication to his family, his friends and his community, but this most honourable of traits is conspicuous in his words and deeds and I for one am grateful.

Clay

INTRO

When I began this project never in my wildest dreams did I think I would take it this far from just writing a story to actually getting as far as putting a book together. I realized as well that certainly I am no English major, but a story teller. Here you will not find everything perfect grammatically for sure. Some sentences will not be perfect English or may not be how a seasoned professional would write. Every ; or – or " , are not necessarily in the right place and in the end, I am OK with that. This is a story that is not perfect and written by an imperfect man. It was important for me to put something together that was much in the same context as to how I speak. To me, it was the story that was the most important.

Those who have spent time in the military will be able to read and understand my ramblings from the Army days with no issues as far as understanding, as it is littered with "army jargon", so throughout I will try to briefly explain what the term means as I go along.

One term I use a lot is Civvy or Civvy Street, which isn't actually a street. While serving, anyone not in the military is referred to as a civvy. Really that was everyone who was not military, so to speak, specifically those who weren't wearing army green. Imagine though, after submitting my draft for review finding out after all these years that I spelt civvy wrong, using only one v. The things you learn.

You'll see many stories that involved drinking, or some drunken event that led to something. It's not that we were always shitfaced, in fact it was quite the opposite. However most times the stories I will tell came about due to some drinking event. Really, wasn't that what many young military lives were, stories that came from some drinking event. It's just that I may have some funny memories that came from some drinking event because there were usually many of us involved. Let's face it, I was young back then.

As I served with the 2nd Battalion of Princess Patricia's Canadian Light Infantry (PPCLI) and have been out of the military for thirty years now, well, to say the least, the transition to Civvy Street has been a journey.

With the help of social media I have reconnected with old brothers from my days of serving and followed many others on various sites. The one thing I see, especially for those getting close to, or retiring, is the difficulty many are having with the transition, and I can confirm, civvies are not like those of us who have lived the military life. Add to the fact that many others are struggling with mental illness and stress, well for some it isn't going to well. I have also seen way too many suicides that are very difficult to hear and read about. We all try to assist or listen, even to those we don't even know, because they are brothers or sisters. I appreciate that more as I get older. Mostly I refer to my brothers, as they were the ones I had the honour of serving with.

I have supported various fundraisers, purchased memorabilia, donated to go funds and other things. Then one day after a rum or nine I decided to write a story which hopefully will give you a laugh as you see my journey through eight plus years of Infantry and then thirty years of Civvy Street where I am, on many days, still back where I started. Infantry. I wanted to write a story of how after all these years I am still very much infantry, through my dealings with Boards, Bosses and especially HR, through the various jobs I have had and how I got here, living the dream in Medicine Hat, Alberta. More importantly, for the troops who read this, I hope it helps those struggling to keep the faith. Once you read about my career, if I can do it, so can you.

It was always my mouth that got me in trouble and really some things just haven't changed. I still live by, "If you don't want the answer, don't ask the question." But sigh....they always asked, and sigh.....I kept answering. It's not like I was mouthy any more than anyone else, but more understanding that if someone asked me a question they should be prepared for an honest answer and not a political one. Some were taken aback by that approach at times, but at least they always understood where I stood or that they may actually get an honest answer. It just wasn't always the answer they wanted to hear. Go figure.

Now that I am north of fifty five years old (fifty four when I started this, and maybe sixty by the time I finish), it is nice to see how strong the brother and sisterhood remains. Let's face it, back in those days we didn't think we'd be around until we were fifty, and sometimes we lived like it. I joked when I finally got here that now that I made it to fifty I just didn't have a plan for that. Now what the hell am I supposed to do?

Looking back, the military was the best awful job I ever had. Of course I don't miss the hard times, as there were many, but I learned to truly understand what a brotherhood is, and I would never have known that without my days in the military.

I will first tell of my journey through my eight plus years serving, how I got there, the places I've been and some stories from along the way. I'll then touch on the journey through Civvy Street and what I learned about HR Departments and its many forms. Keep in mind that the military stories are pretty much all from the 80's when I served. I know the army is different today than it was back then but I guess it's no different than when I was serving and hearing stories from twenty or thirty years prior to that. Decades change, but really, soldiers do not. One thing that is always a constant in the military, there's always a story.

To anybody who has served, and certainly in my day, our HR Department was the grizzled Sgt. who'd say, "Okrainec, sympathy is in the dictionary between shit and syphilis." On Civvy Street I didn't realize there were so many Self Improvement Courses that would eventually lead back to saying to someone, "Go fuck yourself." again.

Maybe through some of these examples it will help you through your next, "Go fuck yourself."

Finally, as this is geared for my military brothers and sisters you'll be seeing the F-verb throughout this story. Everyone has to understand this was the everything word that we started to learn real quickly in basic training. Fuck was an interesting word. It was used in Anger, in Joy, as an Order, just a word to start a Sentence, used in emphasis to pass you something (even if grandma was in the room), a Verb, a Noun, in a Greeting or harsh Exit. You name it, it was the go to word. It took me quite a while to ease it back, but certainly it's still part of the vocabulary, and when required, still a go too.

I've also mentioned first names mostly, and if you are the person, you'll know who you are. I also included some full names of those I wanted to honor as they have passed away or others who were and still are buddies, even if we do not see each other as often as we used to. Well the ones I know of any way. If I spelt your name wrong it wasn't intentional. It should also be noted that almost no one, especially those who were of a higher rank, ever called us by our first names. I have used first names as well to protect some identities somewhat, but in a funny way.

To my family of course, there are many things I have not spoken about during my life in both the military and out in civvy land. Hope you enjoy reading some of the stories and see some of the challenges I have dealt with in my life. I do not talk about you a whole lot in this journey as I needed to write this for me as well. Thanks for being part of the journey. I am nothing without Family and the way I was raised, just along the way I picked up over a thousand brothers who are important to me as well.

So this is for everyone, but especially the troops. I hope it all works out for you, and thank you for your service.

Richard Ernie Okrainec
MCPL 2 PPCLI
VP

PROLOGUE

Hi, it's the same damn writing department. I decided on terms of payment and there was rum in the fridge.

To somewhat understand how I got here I need to go to how I got started. So in a sense it's a diary of events that I realised I was writing for myself and as well hoping my kids could have a laugh one day and understand why I am who I am. Ya who would have thought back in those early days about kids. I mean we had some friends who had kids and we all spoiled them rotten, but for most of us, kids certainly weren't part of the agenda, and now mine are grown up. Yikes, I'm certainly becoming and old bastard.

I was also quite bitter once I left the military for reasons you'll read about later. The military wasn't always the glory and travel. There were many ugly aspects as well. It took me a long time to even go to any form of a military function or reunion. I was finally talked into attending the Base Closure way back of Kapyong Barracks in Winnipeg. I stretched the liver for a few days prior, reluctantly went and it turned out that it was one of the best decisions I ever made. I saw brothers I hadn't seen in many years, of all ranks, and it was difficult just to get to the bar as I was constantly running into people I hadn't seen in many years. There were many a greeting with a big bear hug and followed quickly by telling stories and reminiscing. It was all I could have asked for and more. It was after that I started making an effort to go to events if I could. My close friends knew why I got out, that I was bitter, but they noted they had nothing to do with it. Point made. It really was time to move on.

I say this as I have been lucky to attend a few events over the last few years, other than Remembrance Day which I, or any veteran, just wouldn't miss. The day is important enough to me that when my wife Donia and I were on the road, and the clock turned to 11:00, we pulled over on the TransCanada, hopped out of the vehicle to stand on the side of the road for two minutes of silence. I have managed to recently attend a Beer Call in Edmonton, a get together for the now tear down of our old base in Winnipeg, seeing an old friend in Red Deer, and hooking up with some in Medicine Hat, just to name a few. What I've noticed with some brothers, are those with the same story as me, some worse, some not, but being bitter and just starting to attend these types of events. I also know my struggles of being ticked off are nothing like what the troops are going through today after the rough tours which happened after I departed. The loss of brothers and sisters, the horrors of just what they saw or endured has certainly taken its toll on some. Also to have returned home, only to find out the next battle is with their own Government in court for benefits. I can't imagine those struggles. Many also enjoyed great careers, while still others moved on to different trades or got out like I did. After all these years I have finally put the bad part behind and enjoy the reunions I can. Geez just the last one in Winnipeg I saw four close buddies from those days who I never imagined I would ever see again. Those reunions are more important than holding on to bad memories that I can't do anything about now anyway. Shooting the shit with your buddies is a whole lot more enjoyable than holding grudges.

Also to those struggling to find your way on Civvy Street, we all are who we are. Just be yourself, and you'll find your way. I did not write this to tell you how to adjust, just the story of how I managed to survive through all these years in a world that is so very different than the life we lived in the army. To military people who are starting down this road, or already around the first curve, your life will be vastly different in this world of civvies. I realized when I was just starting to reintegrate back to civilian life that if I wanted to make it and survive it was me who had to somewhat change.

As for me, I came from a small town in Manitoba, Lac du Bonnet. When I say small town, I mean around 1,000 people small. My sister Colleen and I were raised by good parents, Ernie & Ann, who taught us values of a typical small town in Manitoba. I was no different than most, where I heard all the advice and my parents didn't know what they were talking about, then I was on my own, and understood they knew what they were talking about, and I didn't. I grew up with trust, discipline, with good friends, bush parties, sports and a

CHAPTER 1
*CFRS (Canadian Forces Recruit School)
Cornwallis-Nova Scotia-Fall 1980*

From the minute I, or any of the recruits, started training the emphasis was to get the civvy out of us and start turning us into soldiers. There was no coddling and we were all treated the same....like crap. We learned to obey orders, function with no sleep and do many mundane drills that eventually became second nature.

I remember being a slow eater. Well that all changed in basic training as many times we were given minutes to eat for lunch. So we filled our plates, scarfed it back while we were in the line to put the dishes away and then were off running to where we needed to be. The biggest and most important thing was that no one damn well better be late. I learned that if I was fifteen minutes early, that meant I was twenty minutes late. This trait still drives my family nuts to this day. We also learned to eat just about anything when hungry, no matter how awful, and some of the food was all kinds of awful. When I joined I was six foot two inches and 160 pounds. After eleven weeks of Cornwallis I lost ten pounds. So I was skinny as a rake, though in part, I was growing fast. When I went for the sixteen weeks in Wainwright I gained thirty pounds, so the growing out started.

In basic training we all started the same, just long haired civvies known as "Alice" by everyone on base until we got our first buzz cut. We'd be walking around the base and other recruits would be sticking their heads out of the barrack windows and cat call us. After that first head shave I just threw my comb away as I had no hair to look after anyway. It was funny though because after the cut, we didn't recognize each other until we were back sitting at our bunk bed.

The barber messed with us as well during that first buzz cut. I remember they grabbed by buddy Frank, who had a massive afro, brought him to the front of the line, shaved off half his hair and made him have a look. Well after seeing that we knew we were saying goodbye to our hair and grooming the mop that I used to have was no longer required.

There was every walk of life at basic from small town kids to the big city, or those who had a choice of the army or jail, and also those who were a bit older than I was. There was every race, color and creed. There didn't seem to be much for racism as in the eyes of our instructors we were all assholes in need of training.

At the beginning of basic training our platoon started with about 180 recruits in my platoon all sleeping in three or four bunk areas. Once we were weeded out, as in those of us who passed after eleven weeks, we ended with just short of 100 who didn't get re-coursed or failed. Re-coursed meant you we not cutting it and sent to start over again. So as an example, someone may have been four weeks into basic training, but were not doing well and sent back to start again. Once graduated we then went to whatever specific training or career we enlisted for.

Back when I first went to the recruiting office in Winnipeg I wanted to be a Peri (Phys Ed Teacher). I learned later I was going in whatever trade the recruiter was going to put me in. I didn't have a specific skill, other than I was a good athlete, so I was at his mercy and being seventeen I didn't know any better anyway.

We often joked about the recruiter and the methods used that weren't that far off the truth of how we told the story.

"Ok Okrainec, let's start with the eye test. Do you see those three foot letters on the wall?"

"Yes sir I do."

"Ok tell me what it says."

"It says INFANTRY sir."

"Son you were made for the Infantry. Ok time for the hearing test."

He then yelled in my ear, "INFANTRY"

"Did you hear that son?"

"Yes sir. You said INFANTRY."

"Son you were made for the Infantry."

I remembered later that his cap badge was PPCLI so guess where I ended up?

"Listen son, you don't want to be a Peri, you seem to be made for the Infantry. We offer camping, hunting, fishing, money in the bank. What more could you want? You'll get to see the world, a Peri doesn't."

Well that did sound a whole lot better for sure. I loved camping and fishing and sure wanted money in the bank. What could go wrong?

The Canadian Forces had three infantry units throughout Canada. Out west was the PPCLI, the RCR (Royal Canadian Regiment) was the infantry from out east and the Vandoo's were the French battalion based in Quebec of course.

So seeing the names on the list and the fact the Princess Patricia's Canadian Light Infantry had the word Light in it, I felt that just had to be the unit for me. What could go wrong?

So now that this was settled I even got my choice of postings. Out in Victoria (I believe) BC, Calgary or Winnipeg, the three bases of the PPCLI at that time. Well of course I wanted to move away from home and choose it in that order with Winnipeg as my last choice. What could go wrong?

Light....My Ass

So it was finally off to Cornwallis, which really was my first trip on my own, and heading off to basic. It's not like I hadn't travelled as I had been across Canada with my parents, who were good for that, or with relatives. This though was really my first adventure. Well on the way to Cornwallis I had to stay the night in Montreal. This was my first time in Montreal and it was pretty cool. I met up with some other souls who were in the same boat as me, heading off to basic training, and knowing this was our last night of freedom. So of course we decided to go for some drinks. It was suggested we head down to St. Catherine's Ave. which turned out to be where all the strip clubs were. Being a small town guy the closest I would have been to a stripper would have been some guy pissed at a bush party. So now I found out I could pay someone to dance at my table for just $5.00 per dance. What could go wrong?

Well I brought $200 with me to get me to Cornwallis and let's just say I had to borrow cab money to get to the base. Sure was some mighty impressive dancing though.

Once recruits quickly got settled at basic training we all learned in a hurry that life was going to be just a tad different than what we may have been used to. The living without sleep started pretty quick, along with all of the other duties, chores, bunk and kit layout etc. All items had to be arranged perfectly in our locker, folded a certain way, be organized a certain way, every damn day. Crappy tasks such as sewing my name on every piece of clothing that was mine. This included all socks, shirts, pants, t-shirts, underwear and anything else that was now mine. The sewing of the name tags had to be done two stitches up and four across. If anyone did it wrong they were in for a world of hurt. It took longer to sew a nametag on to say.... a t-shirt, then fold and iron it back up perfectly along with everything else and get your locker set up for morning inspection. Only to then, in the morning, have the instructor who was doing the inspecting take everything apart to check if you sewed the names tags on correctly. Naturally we had the honor of repeating this task again for the next morning inspection. I suppose the sewing made sense though, other than the fucking stitching part, as we all had the same green clothes and it would have been pretty damn hard to sort it out during laundry day.

I was in Air Cadets for four years and also attended a summer camp in Penhold, AB, so I knew a little bit about marching and layouts, but this was crazy as we got the opportunity to be yelled at while doing it, at first anyway. Everything had to be ironed perfect, folded perfect, locker perfect, and we even ironed our bed for the morning inspections. Just as you may have seen in a movie, bed tight enough to bounce a quarter. What sucked is we had to make it that way every day. There were some who tried sleeping under their bed so they wouldn't have to make it again, but certainly the training crew saw that fucking trick before and there were many nightly inspections. If someone wasn't actually in their bed, under the covers, but instead sleeping under the bed on the floor, so as to not mess it up, well let's say it didn't go well, even if they were busted in the middle of the night. We all suffered somewhat for the mistakes of others. The bed was then thrown apart along with the locker, and sometimes the bed was chucked out the second floor window. Also remember the many hours shining the heels of my shoes until I was told I could move on to the other part of the shoe, nodding off as I was doing so because of lack of sleep. They kept us awake and we had very long days, and nights.

We were controlled pretty hard and with an iron fist some days. Even the little things like making everyone shave every day, even weekends. Which is why, when soldiers get out of the military, many likely didn't shave for a while, like a revolt. We had this guy, can't remember his name but he was just a hairy Greek. He would always have a 5:00 shadow and be accused of not shaving. Poor bastard had to shave twice a day just so he wouldn't get in shit. And the more he shaved the hairier he got.

There were many lectures and courses daily in rooms I am sure they set at over 30C so you would be even more tired. But man, don't fall asleep or nod off or that person was screwed with some sadistic punishment.

You ironed everything man

We all watched many training videos for sure. Everything from military basics to survival tips. The one I will always remember was the video on how to avoid frostbite. It had two soldiers in a trench and it was very cold. The tips were how to keep warm in a trench to avoid frostbite, especially by moving around. So they had one soldier in the video moving around, wiggling his toes, stomping his feet and such, while the other was the cocky one who didn't move. Shortly after, a battle started and the one who didn't move had frostbite on his toes and couldn't run to get in the fight, while the other was shot in the leg as he got out of the trench. They both went to the hospital and the one who was shot recovered quickly, while the one who froze his toes, his pain was just beginning as all of his toes were dead. They then showed actual footage of a Doctor with a pair of pliers prying and pulling off someone's dead frozen toes. It was gross and all I know is after that when I was in a trench I wiggled my fucking toes!!!

Nights were long, mornings were early. There was lots of running, and recruits weren't allowed to walk on the base, we all had to march. We were also introduced to the basic weapons, the FNC1 (our basic rifle), SMG's (sub-machine guns), the 9mm Pistol and others. Remember being told watch out for the kick of the FN. Well it was just a 3.08 really and anyone who was small town kid went to school with the gun racks in the vehicles. We all hunted. Likely the city kids weren't as familiar.

I likely could do a paragraph just on how much we had to march in some formation or another so I will just say it was never ending march march march, left right left march, march march every day and you'll get the picture.

The short arm inspections weren't a lot of fun either. This is where everyone had to stand, buck ass naked, at attention, while the base Doctor came around to check out whatever needed to be checked out. Though the best story was when we were all ordered to form up for one such inspection. It turned out someone contacted crabs. Geez wonder how that happened? Well they were concerned it would spread, like lice I suppose, so we were all inspected. He found the culprit and asked;

"Well you have them. What's your name son?"

"Crab sir."

Well he hit the floor laughing. Who'd of thought Crab had crabs.

Ya and if anyone was expecting some sort of private accommodations, well they, including myself, were certainly in for a shock. The accommodations were row upon row of bunk beds and the big group showers and bathrooms. Privacy over.

In the first four or five weeks we weren't allowed out, other than maybe church on Sunday, but eventually if we had a good week and didn't get in shit we were then awarded weekend passes. The popular spot was the Green and Gold Club, the recruit bar. Basically as recruits we spent all of our days under wraps. We then made the most of being awarded a mighty four hours of freedom, and of course, we drank as much as we could in four hours, while also meeting some of the female recruits to make a date for Church on Sunday. It's not that many were Church goers, just an opportunity to get out of the barracks for something to do. When the Green and Gold closed troops would try and sneak over to the female shacks, but the MP's (Military Police also nicknamed Meatheads) had them pretty closely guarded. We were shooed away many a time. Ah the romance of Cornwallis, what could go wrong?

There were always rumours that there was saltpeter in the food as well, keep the excitement down, but who knows. We didn't have much time for that anyway.

One thing I found out that wasn't like the movies was the Gas Chamber. The hero doesn't hold his breath and run through shooting at the enemy. He'd be puking what would seem through his eyes, which coincidently is how I felt. That tear gas is nasty shit and they wanted to ensure we got a sniff so that we never wanted to inhale it again, much like a bad tequila story.

Well you may remember the recruiter told me, "Money in the bank." I found out why. We just weren't given any time to spend it. I think I made $500 or $600 per month as a recruit and had over $1,000 in the bank when I was finished.

Basic Training Course 8040

The best part of Cornwallis, other than leaving, was getting our Regular Force, in our case PPCLI, cap badge and getting rid of the Cornwallis Cornflake (the Recruit Cap badge). Once we received the regular forces cap badge we all felt we made it, and were a long ways from the Alice days, which really were just eleven weeks prior, but sure it seemed a lot longer.

½ of my graduating class. Couldn't fit us all in the picture.

So after learning to live with no sleep, how to march, iron everything, some basics of the military, how to use fuck in every version of a sentence, shine floors, clean toilets, make beds, shine shoes and all the other mundane tasks, I made it through and I graduated. It was then a quick Christmas break and right off for sixteen weeks of Infantry training in Wainwright, Alberta.

I remember going home with my uniform on and even going for jogs wearing my combats in the cold Manitoba winter. Just a little gung ho, and oh I had money in the bank. We didn't have strippers back home but we did have a couple bars.

I never did see many of the people I graduated with after that as they went to their trades and we went to ours. Around thirty or forty of us were off to Infantry training, while the others went to their Air Force or Navy trades. Like I said before I was naive to think the BS part was over but the HR Department in Wainwright said fuck even more.

CHAPTER 2

Wainwright Alberta-1981

Wainwright was a different animal, but looking back, a better bad animal. This one was sixteen weeks, so we were at it for quite a while and much longer than Cornwallis. The training was more specific, though at first it was all like basic again and something I wasn't expecting. Not sure what the fuck I was thinking. The overall platoon size was smaller and we lived in H-Huts which were much like small curling rinks. We also started to do more cool training for infantry things. Bigger guns, more ranges, grenades, repelling, using a compass, formations, attacks, section drills and on and on.

In Wainwright the base itself was specifically for Infantry or Combat Arms Training. There was also various Battalion Exercises there that we all went to over the years, but the big difference was it was Combat Arms. No Air Force or Navy, or not very often any way. The Infantry was usually separated as I found out throughout my career. Could be why we didn't play well with others.

As a platoon we were smaller and also closer. Well really we didn't have a choice to be close since we all lived in the same damn room.

For the first few weeks I was doing fine for sure, but around that time our Section MCpl (Master Corporal) left and just my luck on the first inspection with the new Mcpl, he found a speck of mud on my web gear during an inspection and then I was a bag of shit who was screwed. I couldn't do anything right for the next week or so. If you have been through it, well it's not fun, being labeled the flunky. For the first time I didn't think I was going to make it and worried I would either be re-coursed (sent back a week or two with another platoon) or flunked. I even briefly considered going AWOL (Absent Without

Leave, or in other words, without permission). I wasn't really sure how I would turn my fortunes around and the HR Department was unrelenting.

But you never know when your fortunes can change, and sometimes they do when you are just being yourself.

One day, being still young, I had bad acne on my back and had to go get some drugs at the MIR (the Clinic). Well we all knew you didn't want to be labeled an MIR Commando (basically meaning always sick to get out of training) so I tried to hurry and be back before the platoon left for the morning run. I headed over early but the Dr. was late and when I got back the troops were already gone for the run. When I got back to the Shacks (nickname for where we lived) another one of the troops, who also went to the MIR, was faking he couldn't piss for the doc to get out of the run. I instead changed quickly and sprinted out the door. The early part of the run was usually the same and I was a good runner so I boogied hard and ended up catching up to the platoon a couple clicks down the road. The Lt. (Lieutenant) saw me coming up the road behind the troops and yelled, "There is a man coming," and he turned the troops around. My friendly Mcpl asked, "What the fuck is going on Okrainec?" and I explained. I let him know I got hung up at the MIR, when I got back everyone was gone, that I changed and sprinted to catch up. He asked if I could still carry my gear, from which I said, "Of course." He said, "Good man," and after that I wasn't the section flunky anymore.

We did lots of our introduction to Infantry training in Wainwright. Lots of gun ranges, firing hundreds upon hundreds of rounds, like I said bigger guns and bigger ammo, and of course all that camping the recruiter told me about. Going through training in the winter was just a tad cold. The recruiter also didn't mention the digging fucking trenches part, whether through roots, rocks, frozen ground or whatever. It really sucked trying to dig a trench in the winter. We learned to survive in all kinds of weather, especially the cold and that just how important all of our gear was. I also kept wiggling my fucking toes when on sentry in the trenches. Think you may have it tough, well try living in a trench when it's -20C or -30C. We also started some of the hand to hand combat, pugil training (fighting hand to hand with our weapons), which was cool, well cool until you got that first shot in the nuts, then not as cool.

Hold My Beer For A Minute

After the first while we were certainly afforded more free time than Cornwallis and went out most weekends. Weekends in the town of Wainwright sure must have been interesting for the folks that lived there as when recruits went to town it wasn't for shopping. We were hunting.....for liquor.

I even got into my first fight in the shacks. I didn't get into many fights in my life, but sometimes you had to or just didn't have a choice. We had a guy who liked to fight. There was always someone who liked to fight. One night a few of us rolled back in from the bar (what a shock) and came back to him picking on the same guy who wimped out of the morning run a while back. I got into a bit of an argument with him to leave the guy alone as he certainly wasn't going to fight this guy. Well after that I was in his sights. He was following me around and pushing me to go. As this was all taking place late at night, a couple of the troops had heard enough as we were keeping them up. They got everyone up, formed a circle and told us to get it over with so they could get back to sleep. I never considered myself tough, but I wasn't a wimp either. It was over pretty fast. Maybe I was less pissed. He came in and I levelled him in the mouth, he went down. I got on top of him, drifted him a couple more times while his head bounced off the floor and it was over. I realized that's how troops settled HR issues. After that the boys went back about their business. We later shook hands and it was over with. For the most part we didn't hold grudges and I never had an issue with him again, nor he me.

In the end the sixteen weeks went by pretty fast. The majority of us passed, though a few didn't make it. As a group we were also pretty close. Living that close with each other would do that I suppose.

So now it was finally off to the Regular Force as I got set for my third choice of postings……..Kapyong Barracks in Winnipeg.

CHAPTER 3

CFB-Kapyong Barracks-Winnipeg, Manitoba-Summer 1981

So after damn near seven months of being trained I was off to my first posting. Was kind of happy feeling like a soldier and wanting to see what was in store for us with the seasoned soldiers at the base and if the world I lived in would be different.

There were two bases in Winnipeg, Air Command Headquarters, called the North Side, where the Air Force lived over by the airport, and our base, which was pretty much Infantry only, and more the other end of the City. We had some other military attached to us such as mechanics, supply trades, cooks, medics, and the busiest of the trades, the MP's. Ha, we kept those fuckin meatheads hopping for sure.

Keeping us segregated from the rest of the forces well, you can then understand why we didn't play well with others as I mentioned.

Well certainly the Battalion wasn't what I expected. Turned out the troops I graduated with were pretty much A Coy (Company). There may have been ten to fifteen troops in A Coy when we arrived, then we came with an additional thirty to forty. At the base the Battalion strength of troops was just building up and the companies filled up with more troops over the months ahead. Generally the Battalion, at that time, was made up of three Rifle Companies, a Combat Support Company which included Mortar Platoon, Recce Platoon, TOW (the Tank Killers) Platoon, Pioneers (who built things we needed such as say bridges to cross rivers, demolitions among many other things), and an Admin Company with Transport (All the other vehicles), Signals (the Communication Group), Supply and others I likely forget. The battalion would be 400-600 troops when at full strength. An additional Rifle Company was added for Germany. I know I likely forgot some others but you get the drift.

Over the next six months the Battalion and all the companies filled up pretty quick as we were slowly building up for the upcoming Cyprus Tour the following year.

My first Section Commander was a Corporal who I'll say, wasn't made for the infantry. I went on a couple of exercises with him as my fearless leader. Well fuck.....what a disaster. He, after a short while remustered (changed trades) to cook. The fighting troops were likely better off, and the fact we could pretty much eat anything, we didn't have to worry much about him poisoning us.

Looking back, Winnipeg was kind of a blur, as really, we just were not there all that often. In my eight plus years I may have been there for a just a couple. At first, we were forced to live in the shacks (the single quarters) on the base. After a few months we were allowed to move off base if we wanted. So many of us moved off base, just to get away, if only briefly. Mostly, living off base was just to say you had a little bit of freedom. But man, if the shacks could talk. We were just young single army guys and well.....we did some pretty crazy shit for sure. I won't get into many of the things that happened or what I saw. Those are our chuckles. Think of them sometimes and smile. Trying to think of clean story to tell. How about this,

One night my buddy was at a bar, I know that part is a shock (that I had a buddy) and he managed to talk two young ladies back to his room. Problem was he passed out. In the morning he woke up really hung over, just before parade (morning roll call), the girls were gone but they painted him from head to toe in lipstick. He only had about five minutes, so he wiped his face the best he could and tried to hide in the back ranks with lipstick still on his ears and neck and the rest of his body. Geez from guys hanging from their door knob via their dog-tags, passed out, because that's where they had their room key, to... well...I'll leave it at that.

As a soldier everyone also learned really fast that you just don't pass out around the boys. You may just wake up missing things, like your eyebrows. Ah life on the base. Like when Wild Bill bought a jeep, then decided he needed to test the roll bars on the Parade Square. You know everyday stuff.

In prep for us soon to be doing a tour in Cyprus, we were in a heavy training schedule. Driver Wheel (Jeeps, 2 ½ Ton, 5-ton trucks, or obviously anything with wheels), Driver Track (the Armoured Personnel Tracked Vehicle-APC), Machine Gun (50-Caliber), Sigs (Signals, Radios and Codes) and on and on. Initially it was mostly the basic courses, and the next go of courses we could or would advance to more specific things such as Mortars, Recce, Anti-Tank-Tow, and others courses, which was pretty cool looking back. When we were doing the classroom everyone was on the base doing the same thing in their particular courses. When the field portion (basically meaning it was off to the woods) came we'd spread out and didn't see many of the boys for weeks at a time if they were on a different course.

Also, like any unit, we did lots of drill, marching and parades including drill teams and competitions. This happened everywhere we were posted, and was part of being infantry. Prior to leaving for both Cyprus and Germany the Battalion conducted the Freedom of the City March in downtown Winnipeg. It was pretty damn cool marching down Portage and Main as a Battalion. The Freedom of the City usually took place when the Battalion was being deployed, such as when we were off to Cyprus and then again to Germany.

We always had some fucking inspection of some form all the time. Whatever the uniform of the day was, our summer or winter kit, weapons, vehicles, and so on. There was roll call and inspections each morning for those who lived in the shacks especially. These inspections seemed more to find out just who made it back from whatever drunken adventure they were on. There were still room inspections but not as often and more to make sure it was neat. I filled pretty much my entire ceiling with the sexy posters of the day, Farrah, Bo Derek, Kate Jackson and others. The Officer or Senior NCO would come in, look up, walk around and say, "Room is good, really good." Never failed an inspection.

We certainly had some fun while living in the shacks many a day. Tuesday night it was Barny and Binnie`s room for euchre and then Mork and Mindy. When I roomed with Perry Batchelor it was the 2:00 AM runs for a hoagie at 7-11. We could stay on the base and if you had no money fun could still be had. There were always three squares a day at the Mess Hall. No one would starve. For us, there was also the Junior Ranks Club (for those ranked Master Corporal and below) where the drinks were cheaper than downtown. So of course that's where we started, or got to enjoy some pretty good concerts and shows at the club. Each lunch there was also a stripper. There were always boys at the Club. The boys looked after each other, even if some of them were crazy fuckers.

There was also a Senior NCO's Club for Sgt.'s and above, and an Officer's Mess for all of the Officers, obviously. So pretty much each rank structure had their own establishment. This also kept the various ranks separate so people wouldn't get hammered and want to beat up their Sargent or Officer, or vice versa.

When in garrison things were pretty routine and mundane. Most did PT (Physical Training) as a Platoon every morning. This for the most part was a morning run. How hard the run was depended on who was in charge. The only rule was…Don't Miss PT. Anyone could go and do whatever the fuck they wanted but don't miss PT. Many of the boys, including myself, had those right out of 'er runs for sure. The kind where the sweat is running down the crack of your ass and your T-shirt was soaking wet with sweat after 200 meters of running. But you didn't miss PT.

So one day we are all running along and getting close to heading off the base. So if you can picture a Platoon of twenty to thirty guys all dressed the same with their maroon T-Shirts and shorts, all in a formation, and heading off for the four to eight miles we'd run most days. Then as we were moving along I thought I was hearing something weird, but clop clop clop was the sound from the back of the Platoon. I looked back and there was Russ, still in his jeans, cowboy hat and cowboy boots, coming from wherever, but he didn't miss PT. The LT. just said, "Russ (I use first names for stories like these as we were never called by our first name), what the fuck are you doing, get the fuck out of here." He didn't get in trouble though and we laughed our asses off. Good effort

We didn't always have the swiftest guys either. One day this Sgt. had had enough with a truck being broken down and he took it out on a Corporal.

So he barked to him, "You take the fucking truck over to maintenance and I don't fucking want to see you until the fucking thing is fixed."

So he did what he was told. The next few days he wasn't on parade and no one knew where he was. On the fifth day he showed up and they wanted to charge him (where you went to a Military Trial, depending on the charge, but usually resulted in fines or extra duties for small shit) with being AWOL but he just said;

"You said not to come back until the truck was fixed. They just finished."

What could they do, to the letter he did what he was told, and didn't get charged. Geez why didn't I think of that?

I also had a Sgt. at first who was kind of gung ho. Well not kind of, he was. When we were in garrison we did lots of drill and weapons inspections as I noted. Many of the times when we signed out a weapon for inspection we didn't get our weapon, just a weapon. So one day we were getting inspected and the Sgt. decided he was going to inspect weapons. He started taking mine apart and it was filthy. He started chewing me out for showing up with a weapon like this.

I said, "It's not my weapon Sgt."

"Who's fucking weapon is it Okrainec?"

"Well, it would be your weapon Sgt."

I got through the rest of the inspection.

I also learned early not to volunteer for things, but many of us would get tricked into some task. The Sgt. would ask, "Ok who here likes hockey?" I fired up my hand because I liked hockey. "Ok then, well skate up to headquarters and deliver this memo."

There were many of these and over time we all would learn not to get tricked or else we'd be getting some chore we didn't want to do.

The thing was, wherever the military had a base, the troops would spend every nickel wherever we hung our hat. Whether it was a bar, a lounge or a restaurant, a nearby grocery store, everyone shopped there. That's just the way it was. Bases really helped the local economy, even if some businesses didn't appreciate it. When the plan was a night on the town of course things always started at the Junior Ranks as the liquor was cheaper, but the main hangouts in those days were Pepper's Lounge across the street and The Grant Hotel, the bar a little ways down the road. The army guys were in the majority there. Sometimes there would be fights, other times just a good time.

Well this one weekend, I wasn't there, there was a big fight at The Grant. Army guys against civvies. On Monday the owner of the hotel got a hold of our base and told the CO (Commanding Officer) or someone at headquarters that we were barred for a year from The Grant. We had a parade and were informed as such. Bummer, we had to find a different bar, but there were many options in Winnipeg. I guess around a month later he contacted the base to say we could come back. The CO said, "No, you said a year." Guess he was losing quite a bit of money, but the CO wanted to make a point. If the establishment didn't want us, fair enough, we'll take our money elsewhere. As for us, we were army guys, we adapted.....especially for liquor.

In those early days the cool training I got to do was taking the Driver Track Course in Resolute Bay. We flew way up north in Herc Aircraft, all us troops, our gear and the APC's. The course was in the summer for about eight weeks and up there it was twenty four hours of daylight that time of year.

Well the chalk (the flight) I was on got fogged out and we couldn't land in Resolute and ended up in a place called Rae Point for a day or two, wherever that was. It was another construction area of some sort up north in the middle of nowhere. Well we loved it just for the food. No awful hay box meals here that we were accustomed to. The roast beef hung over the plate, eat all you want, a games room to pass time. We were living......well more comfortable than we were used to. We all knew we were heading for a life of outdoor living in module tents for a while, so we all took the comforts when we got them. After a day or so we were off to join the rest of the troops and landed to commence the course.

Well Resolute Bay really is in the middle of no-where-ville, well not that anyone would expect some sort of a metropolis, but there was a village on the other side of the bay from where we were camped in module tents. We all slept on cots. Camp also included a mess area (kitchen) and lounge, which of course we could have drinks when training was over. Go figger. There was also a town/camp kind of where there was a regular bar. We would truck in there sitting in the back of 2 ½ tons. So one night I was ready to go to the bar with the boys, rode in the back of the truck bouncing around for a half an hour, get to the bar and I get ID'd. I was eighteen, but low and behold the drinking age up there is nineteen. "Sorry you can't come in." Well now what the fuck do I do, just wait outside. Well I must have made good puppy eyes because he felt sorry for me and let me in. It's not like there are a lot of police wandering around up there.

We knew we were in the wrong fucking trade compared to the civilian construction guys as these guys were getting an extra $100 per hour for isolation pay. On top of the $125 per hour they were making. We were getting $6 per day extra in field pay and eating hay box meals. Bastards.

Way up north there are no trees and your compass doesn't work as we were very close to the Magnetic North Pole. This meant the compass didn't point north, as the needle just spun in circles. And to make it even more interesting all of the terrain looks the same, rolling hills and rock. So needless to say it was quite difficult to navigate. I remember doing one patrol which took all day and we ended up going in one big circle. Sure would be a bugger in the dark. Sometimes when we were on the long patrols or moves we'd have the Inuit guide with us as they could find their way around.

Track Course Resolute Bay and some findings

I did see a lot of firsts up there. Old plane crashes, bog, muskox, an Eskimo village, old monuments and on and on. Wish I would have taken more pics, but that was the story of my life in the military. When we did get out for drinks we'd come out of the bar at around 2:00 AM and the sun would be noon high. Was cool, and hey, gave us more stamina.

Of course some of the boys did the polar swim. There was a Company event where a big hole was cut in the ice and a few jumped in. I was having none of that for sure. Was cold enough already. It may have been summer up there, but it wasn't that damn warm.

I also remember the village located across the bay having a small whale or very large fish of some sort anchored near the shore and they would come out and cut a piece off to eat. Natural freezer I suppose.

The driving around the countryside was awesome, especially all of the scenery. The water was so clear we had to be careful crossing small rivers as they may look three feet deep but were closer to twenty.

One night after a long day of driving, we set up camp. When away from Base Camp each Section slept in ten man tents and we all used our issued air mattresses. We were woken up in the morning by a Mcpl who noted we probably would want to get up slowly. Turns out our fearless Cpl leader set us up in a riverbed and it filled up overnight and we were all floating around on our air mattresses. We were still mostly dry until some dumbfuck from the Reserves, who were in training with us long before the Reserves did much with the Reg Force, got wet, the water was cold, and he freaked out a bit and tipped us all over. Now it was fucking cold. Dumbshit. We spent the better part of the day trying to dry our gear. Needless to say we didn't like him very much.

Later, in a form of karma, he was in a pickle we wouldn't want to be in. You see when in the middle of nowhere you set up basic comforts, like where to take a crap. So our set up was four stakes of rebar surrounded by a canvass tarp. Everyone knew to be careful not to crap in the hood of our parka or our dangling pants. But more importantly don't hold on by the rebar while squatting to do some business. So when he was doing his business, he of course was holding on by the rebar. Dumbshit. It of course gave way and he fell in the shithole. So there he was, pants down to his ankles, boots and hands up, stuck in the shithole. We didn't provide him much help and let him figure it out. We laughed our asses off.

We also found the polar bear license plates pretty darn cool as well, and had a bad habit of taking them. So one day the CO or some Senior Officer from the area went to headquarters to complain about us taking the license plates from the vehicles and demanded we stop. When he came out later, well, his were gone too. If anything we were efficient. So needless to say, shortly after that it was a kit inspection and all the license plates were retrieved. For some reason a bunch of people took up smoking from soap stone pipes, or so I heard. Hey we were Infantry.

Summer In Resolute Wasn't That Damn Warm

I'm really glad we got to do that training up there. It's a landscape most people will never see. It would sure take some getting used to in the winter when it was dark twenty four hours per day.

After Resolute it was back to Battalion and later that fall it was off to exercise RV 81 at CFB Gagetown, New Brunswick. This was a large training base and one I, and many others, would frequent in our careers. It was my first big exercise with many of the different forces there. All in all it was an ok exercise. Max the Ax, our CSM (Company Sgt.-Major) made it more difficult having our company clear the bush area to more of a parking lot just for something to do. That was also the last exercise we had with our fearless Corporal leader. Was better for all of us he went to another trade. I also found out to that the C2 Magazine Vest (the C2 was the rifle with a bi-pod and more ammo and you were required to wear a type of bra on your chest with the 30-round magazines in the bra) sucks when you are sweating your ass off and the sweat rusts the magazines, or so I found out during a fucking kit inspection one morning.

The right to be the C2 gunner, which was a bigger weapon with more ammo, was usually, "Hey you, you're fucking tall, you're the new C2 gunner."

The C2 with Cleaning Kit and Magazine Bra you wore across your chest

I was still young so the training was alright. This was also the first time going long periods without a shower. I also got some trench foot in the arches of my feet, where my arches both had deep cracks and broke apart and bled when I walked. It sure hurt like a bugger especially when it was dry, but we were trained to just carry on. No pain no gain right? I also had my middle finger squished by the cam (camouflage) poles. Vehicles had the large poles attached which made it easier to set up the camouflage of the APC when we parked. Well the top of my finger was squished by the poles bouncing around while we were driving. It was the kind where I had to get a needle through the nail to relieve the pressure. I must say nothing felt so good than seeing that blood squirt out when the Doc put the hot needle through my nail to release the pressure. My nail however hasn't grown back properly since.

Guess who won the toss-Sometimes you just has to cross the river

People got weird shit living in the field. Had one guy who was having trouble hearing for a couple of days so he finally went to the Dr. Turns out there was a spider nesting in his ear. The boys made a make shift shower in which a drum of water was hanging and was supposed to tip water for the shower. Just a small problem though as it wasn't built properly and the drum crashed on to the guy showering. We also learned very fast, be careful dumping a load in a port-a-potty. Seen a few guys get it turned over with the door down. The mosquitos could also be brutal living in the bush. We were issued mosquito nets that we could wear over our head while sleeping but those bastards could be relentless. Nothing was as great as seeing a flock of dragonflies show up. The mosquitos buggered off when that happened. We also had that insect repellant that had major deet in the mixture that I am pretty sure wouldn't be legal in these days. We liked it more because that stuff was the only way to get that damn cam paint off our face.

Because grunts don't use roads

But other than that we lived a completely normal life.

I also got one of those camp duties you may only see in the movies, filling large garbage cans peeling potatoes. We all got that type of duty. Think I filled three drums with potatoes, along with a couple other guys to feed the troops. Those types of duties sucked, but we all had to do them.

The one thing I learned in a hurry was the dislike of the Vandoo's. Not that they did anything to me personally, but we had all of the older gear and kit while they rolled in and around with everything new. Geez I wonder at that time where our PM's were coming from.

After six or eight weeks we were done and it was back to Battalion.

We did a lot of training right in Winnipeg back in those early days. Back then the base was kind of at the end of the City in that part. There was even bush in the back we could train in and we used to do our ten miler runs down Taylor Ave. as it was just a gravel road with not much traffic. The City has sure built up since those days, to the point now that they are tearing the old place down.

One particular memory I enjoy was giving the civvies a treat one day when the choppers showed up across the street in the fields of Lipsett Hall right across from the base. This area, which was part of our base, housed the gym and all the sports fields. They landed, we got on, went up about 100 or 150 feet then repelled out. That was pretty cool doing for sure, especially in the City.

And out the door we went

I was also in when version one of Trudeau was in power, so not much money was being spent on the Military for sure. We usually didn't have blanks (pretend bullets) when we were on exercise and would yell, "Budget, budget budget" when shooting. I heard that still goes on from time to time.

We didn't ride trains in Canada to exercises. We either drove or flew. In Germany we took trains too many exercises which I note later in this story. But I did get to ride one back with some of the boys. We were doing a winter exercise in Wainwright. Think it was called Rapier Thrust. I don't remember much about the exercise, other than it was really fucking cold, and we lived outside the entire time. When the exercise was over the tracks were being taken back to Winnipeg via train and Len Barr who was a Sgt., great guy, asked a few of us to help out loading and unloading the tracks and to ride the train back. I remember it was in and around my birthday so I would miss it, but he needed help and I didn't mind. We'd be back a day or two later than the rest of the troops, but we got to ride in the caboose, which was something I hadn't done before. Of course he also loured us with the left over Navy Rum rations. So we loaded all the vehicles on the train and started back. There were five of us in the caboose along for the ride. Of course we were getting shitfaced, after loading everything on the train of course, as we didn't have to drive and the trip took almost two days to get back to The Peg. So in the middle of the trip we were doing about 50 mph and all off a sudden the train brakes were slammed on and we came to a sudden stop, well sudden as far as trains go. Len happened to be standing up with his rum and went flying and rolling from the back of the caboose to the front and hit the wall. He quickly jumped up and said, "I didn't spill a fucking drop!!" and we looked and his rum was still full. One of the train engineers, a short time later, came banging on the door. He was pissed off as he thought we pulled the emergency brake. He whipped the door open to chew us out, saw five drunken army guys looking at him, and did an about face and buggered off. Turned out the brakes froze and that caused the train to do an abrupt halt. We laughed our asses off. Especially how fast he buggered off scared shitless.

If you ever get to do this type of train ride though, and you get a chance, do it. It's pretty nice riding through the Canadian countryside looking at the scenery from a train for sure. We got back to Winnipeg at the train yards on the east end of the city. Told Len I would just hitchhike back to my place figuring someone would pick me up. There was nowhere to make a phone call so off I went winter gear and all. Well not one person stopped to give me a ride so I had to fucking hump about ten miles in the winter, with all my gear, back to my place. Mmmmm...should have taken the ride as it was pretty cold. Dumbfuck. But in those days we were prepared to walk anywhere, likely these days too. We just did it.

Somewhere as I rolled into 1982 I was on the shortened version of the Section Commanders Course as they would need a batch of NCO's (Non-Commissioned Officers) for our upcoming tour to Cyprus. This was the first Leadership Course to get promoted to Mcpl. It was a shorter course than the normal sixteen weeks but instead eight to ten weeks. Some of the older Mcpl's weren't happy that we got to do a shorter course than they had to do, but what were we supposed to do, not take it. It was still difficult enough. We all taught various classes and drill and were graded, and also did a portion in the field leading patrols and mostly compass training. If you couldn't operate a compass you weren't going to pass. It was cool when we did the field portion, as it turned out we were in the woods just a few miles from my hometown. Not that I partied that damn deep in the woods. It was also really cold, about -25C for the entire field portion. Waking up in the morning with my boots frozen solid with no bend while knowing I still had to put those fuckers on. It's also why we did so much winter training, to work and survive in extreme weather. There was nothing more appreciated than the stove watch through the night in the ten man tents as we all took shifts keeping the stove going to keep the frost line down while the others slept. There was also no better feeling than climbing into our badass sleeping bag after a day in the cold. It was made for the cold. What sucked though was when we had to get out of it in the morning.

As for all the winter survival training we endured, well you know because we were going to Cyprus where they didn't have winter and we were going to Germany where they had next to no winter, compared to Manitoba. We all learned to survive hauling that tent sled in snow shoes to get to where we were going. I think it was just because, and to toughen us up.

In the infantry we learned to appreciate the little things. Like getting something warm to eat or drink, the night shift in the ten man tent with a stove going to keep us warm, or a shower, which many times didn't happen for days at a time. We learned the importance of the old hygiene in the field, but let's face it, that underwear was being retired at the end of the ex. No matter what memory we may have had with it. In the end we all stunk like a dead skunk on the TransCanada.

After I got through the course I wasn't promoted yet but became a 2 IC (2nd In-Command) of a Rifle Section. The first opportunity in hoping to get promoted was going down to Fort Reilly Kansas for training with the Big Red One, who were made somewhat famous as a movie was made about this unit back in the 60's I think.

The problem I encountered however was I was a decent shot and made the Rifle Team, who obviously wouldn't be going down south. It would be hard to get promoted if I didn't go to Fort Reilly. I had a Sgt. tell me as much and said, "Okrainec you better make sure you don't shoot very well on the ranges with the Rifle Team." I was to shoot bad so they would send me back to the company to go on the training. So I did. I made sure I shot badly on the ranges. Well the Sgt. in charge of the Rifle Team knew something was up when they looked at my targets and saw my grouping of rounds were all over the place. He knew I wasn't that horrible of a shot. I then explained why I was shooting badly and they were quite reasonable, but noted I could still get promoted if I stayed on the Rifle Team. He told me if I felt better going south to the States I could go back to the Company to do the training, and he accommodated me. His understanding was greatly appreciated and I went back to the Rifle Company and headed south for training.

CHAPTER 4
Fort Reilly, Kansas And Back-1982

Training with the Americans was quite an experience being it was my first view of them up close. I found out quite quickly that the US Military was much different than ours. The amount of equipment they have is unreal. They are massive. There were more soldiers posted in Fort Reilly, than we had in our entire Armed Forces, by a lot. They were trained well enough, from my observations in working with the infantry guys we dealt with, but I felt our skills were more in-depth. By that I mean we were trained in everything, while for the most part they were experts or trained in one thing.

An example I remember was bouncing around sitting in the back of one of their tracks and it blew a track. So we were waiting for them to start fixing it and he told us it wasn't his job, he was just the driver, and someone would be along shortly to fix it. With us you got the hell out and fixed it and got back in the game. We all fixed and pounded track. I can't say it was like that everywhere, but it was in this case.

Of course the first night we hunted for a bar. Being I was under twenty one, I wasn't allowed in the general bars, but they had bars for troops under the age of twenty one, as many soldiers were just that in both Armies. So I survived, barely. A big crew of us found a bar and started pounding the weak American beer. Along the way, after a few pints, we realized they were only playing disco music. So after a few loud rounds chanting, "Disco Sucks," a big African American came up to us and asked what we were doing there. Turns out we were in a blacks only bar. Once they found out we were Canadians everything was cool and it was a fun night. This however was my first brush with the racial divides that still exist with our southern neighbours. Not that we don't have it, just not as prominent back in the 80's.

So as we started to prepare for our training and getting a favor from the Rifle Team to release me back to the Company for a better chance of training and working towards a promotion, what did I reward them with?

I went to Kansas and forget my fucking Web Gear back in Winnipeg. Dumbfuck.

Kind of need your Web Gear since you have to wear it

I'm supposed to be a soldier, how the fuck do you forget your Web Gear? Which, coincidently is exactly what my CSM asked, with a lot more fucks involved, which included at the end, "Okrainec, if you ever want to be promoted you better get your head out of your ass." Dumbfuck

Well I deserved that and am a believer in taking your medicine. I was lucky one of our troops was hurt and I borrowed his web gear for the duration. When I got back to Canada I found that I left the Web Gear under my bed. Dumbfuck

The training there was on a very large scale compared to what we were used to for sure. I also realized that there would be times, being infantry, that we would be completely and utterly fucked and out gunned. Sitting in a trench during an attack and seeing the A10`s bearing down on our position, or a large Tank Group approaching is an uneasy feeling. There wouldn't be much a 7.62 round was going to do. Not much any of us could do without support.

Better duck grunt

Ya I'll take you out with my 7.62 rounds

When we were preparing for the field we were issued snake bite kits. Also told when we woke up to make sure we shook our boots out in case snakes were sleeping in them. WTF!!! I fuckin' hate snakes with a passion.

One time during an attack I was laying in the prone position and a fuckin' snake slithered by. Let's just say I wasn't examining if it was a rattlesnake or a water moccasin. I don't care how quiet and stealthy we were supposed to be; I was up and fucking out of there running my ass off.

So we were doing what we do, walking and training in the woods. After a long hump, we were taking a rest. I put my helmet down and saw a bunch of pot plants. I thought it was cool, then I stood up and there were acres upon acres of the stuff growing wild. Five to six feet tall nicknamed, "Kansas Killer." So of course we changed our cam pattern and put pot plants in our helmets and other areas.

During one of the major exercises I had a buddy who was with a track that had broken down and the Yanks forgot about them for three days. I asked him what he did and if he was worried. He said, "No actually, we had food, water and Kansas Killer. We got by."

I mentioned we got to do cool shit. Right near the top was the chopper flying down there. We were being moved via chopper to prepare for an attack. Well the pilots were Vietnam Vets and we flew tree top with the doors open at a high rate of speed, dropped off, and they were gone. Was pretty neat, but I made sure I held on for sure. Then not long after we were dropped off another group of choppers came in and started dropping off the enemy force. The issue was, they fucked up and dropped them off where we were, instead of where they were supposed to go. Needless to say the fight was on pretty quick. We were using the Miles Gear, just like the Clint Eastwood movie Heartbreak Ridge. We also found out a bunch of them were cheating bastards and didn't put the batteries in. So there were some good fights about that, including a rifle butt stroke here and there.

When we were in the field, showers were few and far between as I mentioned. One such day I was walking over for lunch through the bush and someone in front of me snapped a branch back and it caught me square in the eye. Right away I couldn't see. The medic had a look and I had a scratched cornea and was blindfolded and taken back, via jeep, to base to the hospital.

So now I don't know where I am, I'm blindfolded, but know I am sitting in the waiting room of a hospital with whoever else was in there. I then start to hear groaning and shuffling and quiet complaining. Well it turns out I hummed pretty bad, as I hadn't had a shower for quite some time. Shortly after that I was guided to a private room, where I could enjoy the stench all to myself. Well I guess I left my mark anyway. As for the eye, I had to wear a patch for a couple of weeks and didn't have full vision for about six months.

When we were in garrison things were uneventful, but we were allowed to buy liquor for about $5.00 a 40 oz. Well we made good use of the spare time mostly playing cards and telling stories. It was also where I started smoking just because most everyone else did.

The Yanks also took us to a ball game at Kaufman Field in Kansas City for a game against the White Sox, though quite a few wouldn't remember who were even playing. What a day that was. Lots of fun and ummmmmm........just a little bit of liquor. We were lit from the bus ride in which was a two or three hour ride.

My one buddy Ted Saikkonen and I agreed that he'd buy the beer and I'd buy the hotdogs, as they were the same price. All I remember is that I bought twenty four hotdogs. With our large group let's just say if you were sitting behind us in the stands you weren't getting any beer, at least from the beer vendor, as we'd buy the rack. They even showed us in the stands on the Jumbotron, even though they noted we were from Wainwright. We cheered pretty hard. All in all it was a fun crazy day.

One of the bigger exercises I remember was being enemy force for The Big Red One, who were training and soon off to Germany. They expected us to attack at first light but whoever was in charge of us fucked them up. We walked the better part of the day and attacked them in the middle of the afternoon and caught most of them sleeping. We severely kicked their ass as they had next to no sentries and most of them were having an afternoon nap. After this their CO declared victory and that they were ready for Germany. Ya what the fuck ever.

In the end it was great training with our allies, and then it was back to home base, where of course I found my Web Gear, under my bed. Dumbfuck.

Not much longer after we got back to Winnipeg I was fortunate enough to get promoted to Master Corporal. So now I was a nineteen year old Master Corporal, and the good and bad adventures of being a leader began. Problem was many of the older Mcpl.'s weren't much help, at least those who didn't believe we all should have been promoted. Ya whatever. I just learned to live with it, and eventually it just went away.

Once back in Winnipeg I still had the regular crew that came with me many weekends to party in my hometown. They became part of the furniture and my parents for the most part loved it. Ted, Barny, Binnie, Clay, Greg, Spanky, Jim and many others. Of course we were all young and gung ho. There always was someone who wanted to pick a fight with one of them and usually it was a bad idea. Barny and this other guy from my hometown had such an event that didn't last very long. Barny was taking a piss and was pushed from behind by someone who wanted to go. So without missing a beat, Barny, with his dick flopping around, beat the crap out of him with his head pounding of the sink a few times. Barny then zipped up and left. So much for that. We tried for the most part to avoid the fighting stuff. We just wanted to have some fun. But much like us, there was always someone who wanted to fight.

In Manitoba there was a social pretty much most weekends in many towns, including my hometown. If you are not from Manitoba, basically these were dances for some event, a Wedding Social, a Fundraiser, or any event like this. One year a bunch of us went to the Halloween Dance. I went as a flasher. Had the large army green coat, bought a ring of garlic sausage and sewed a large chunk to my gym shorts. Later, I had these witches harassing me until I flashed them and they laughed their asses off. The last thing I remember was doing the costume parade and being on the center of the dance floor and the three witches were eating my sausage. I woke up in the morning with a little piece left, and another chunk hanging by the skin. Well wasn't that a good night.

Those who know me know I loved fastball. Being posted in Winnipeg I still played with my hometown team and usually Barny, Binnie and Ted would come to the games, four in the Cab of my truck, and off to the various small towns which were in the league I played. It was a summer of fun that still brings a smile to my face. Did some crazy shit on those road trips from the base for sure, but we managed to survive.

The road trips were big adventures, as it may have only been an hour trip back to Winnipeg, but we needed to drive in shifts with the non-drivers having a nap before we got back to parade to survive whatever the army would have us doing that day. So it was Barny's turn to drive the first shift. I had the truck.

I woke up and we were on the side of the road and Barny is out front having a piss. Ted was with us.

"Hey Barny, where are we?"

"Fucked if I know Ernie, but we're out of gas."

Turns out he drove around Winnipeg and we were about an hour from the US border. It's 3:00 AM and parade is 7:00ish. Fucker. Flagged someone down, got going an hour or so later, and it was high speed back to base so as to not miss parade. We didn't want to be like Russ in those cowboy boots. So I had to run eighteen red lights in the City, but we made it back in time for parade.

Another time, it was my turn to drive, when just outside of Winnipeg I was passing someone and fell asleep.........I woke up in the ditch with snow flying over the hood, Barny's head whapping off the window, and I steered back on the highway and continued passing the guy like nothing happened, you know.... nothing to see here. Barny didn't move a muscle. Once back on base and on my way to parade I noticed something and looked at the grille of my truck and there was a duck in the grille. Mother fucker. Poor duck, imagine his last thoughts, sitting on the ice in the ditch then, "What the fuck is that?"...squich. Poor duck. Someone was also looking out for us some days.

Yet another time, four in the cab, speeding, open liquor, no registration and we get pulled over right about halfway home before a little town called Libau. Somehow Barny talked them out of arresting me and told them I was going to Resolute Bay the next day. So instead they towed my truck and left us on the side of the highway, but didn't charge us. Fuckers took the liquor though. We walked to Libau and played pool until my buddy's mom, who owned the local taxi, came to get us. Good timing as we had won the pool table and the locals were pissed off. Mom and dad bailed my truck out of the compound while I was away and sent me a picture. Was nice of them for sure, but if that truck could talk they might have taken it back to the compound.

I really won't get too much into the camping adventures as I mentioned earlier but you can make your own conclusions. Like the night Spanky stole the rental vehicle from us at Old Pinawa and came back 800 miles later, which was 600 miles over the free miles limit. You know, a non-drinking kind of weekend.

When you were the one with a vehicle, from which I was one, you did much of the driving to get around. Obviously everyone couldn't afford their own wheels. As Assiniboine Park was close to the base it was a great hangout in the summer. Many of the boys would enjoy the park, games of Football or Frisbee and some drinks. We enjoyed the Park as we ran through there most days. Well a bunch of the boys wanted to go and I had the truck. I set the record for most in the cab of the truck at seven people, it took three of us to drive, as I had a stick shift, and another twenty or so in the back and it was off to the Park. The Police saw us and just shook their heads. In the end we weren't hurting anyone.

As we were in the field a lot, a big part of what we looked forward too was getting a care package or letters sent to wherever we were, usually deep in the bush somewhere. The care packages were even more welcomed when we were in some far away land and they didn't have normal things we may like, like certain chips brands, treats, food or whatever. My parents always sent me Klik in the package. We'd get magazines, cookies, chocolates, chips, canned food favorites, you name it. Of course you would have to share with the boys who were around, but you also kept the good stuff to yourself. We all loved mail day, then would start sniffing around as to who got what.

So now it was somewhere in the summer of 1982 and we were preparing for a winter tour in Cyprus. October 1982 – March 1983.

CHAPTER 5
Cyprus-Winter Tour Oct 1982- Apr 1983

Preparing for Cyprus wasn't super difficult as it was mostly getting ready for various OP (Out Post) duties. Sentry duty. Wasn't sure what to think about this tour, but it was a UN Tour overseas, so I was kind of looking forward to it. That was until a day or two before leaving we were informed my friend and brother Jessie Prins had died there. Doesn't matter how, it was still hard. It was one of those times we were wondering why we were called on Parade, then they announced the news. He was my first friend who had died and was kind of hard to take. I went through it all with Jessie from Basic to Battalion, so it was really sad. You just think, "Geez any day could be the day I suppose."

Cyprus, as far as the zone we patrolled, was called the Green Line, and was for the most part pretty quiet. The Green Line was basically the line down the middle which separated the Greeks and Turks. In the City, Nicosia, where we were, the Line was basically each side of the street in spots, while in the country it could be a couple miles wide. The Greeks and the Turks weren't fighting at the time, though every once in a while one would kill the other. Seemed sometimes it was more about keeping the UN there on the island. I mean think of the amount of money we spent on the island, like all of it, as did each nations soldiers. When we managed to get time off let's face it, the beaches were the Mediterranean.

Right off the bat though, I got a bit of a reality check. I was on a walking patrol on the line when suddenly I heard a weapon cock and saw a barrel of a gun pointed at my head. Being it was dark I did what we were told to do and shinned the flashlight on my beret and said, "UN." He lowered the barrel and

I carried on. I think they did that to mess with us, as at that point there wasn't anybody else cruising the line, especially in the middle of the night. Didn't honestly think too much about it until later, not that it fucked me up or anything, just we let things roll off and carry on, but also how quick the end could come.

My group was housed out of Ledra Palace in Nicosia. It wasn't a Palace, probably was before the war, but was more than comfortable, and indoors, not the bush. It was a very large hotel that housed many of us. About half of us lived there. The other half of the Battalion were housed a little ways from us in CML (Camp Maple Leaf). For those of us living in Ledra Palace the problem was, most of the Officers and Senior NCO's lived there as well, so we didn't get away with much. Most of what we needed was there and we all ran into all various ranks quite a bit, well not quite a bit, but daily.

My job, at first, was a Line NCO, so I got to patrol the line and the OP's, for the most part, in a jeep. Drove from OP (Out Post) to OP to check up on things, bring supplies or help changing the shifts. Each shift on the OP was eight hours and all we did was rotate from OP to OP, and there were several OP's with shift work. In between we got some time off. It was a decent job. I was a new Mcpl and had a Sgt. that I rarely saw over the six months. Usually it was only when I was in trouble, ok, maybe I did see him quite a bit when I started messing up a lot. But he wasn't around very much to help for sure. Certainly was frustrating, especially since I was running things in his absence. He spent more time chasing the Mute (a legend in the Cyprus times) than being with the troops. Certainly the boys from that era would know who the Mute was. My Sgt. would only roll in when required, then when things weren't going well I'd be in shit for him not doing his job.

And throughout the six months, sometimes in shit we got. This must have been due to the fact that we could get drinks for about 10 cents. I could likely do a chapter just on the shit I was in, but I'll save some trees. In the end it was all on me and the dumb choices made with one too many drinks, and I only had myself to blame. Usually it was what came out of my mouth.

The funny thing was there was another Mcpl who looked like my twin, and of course his name was Ernie as well. Well he got called in quite a bit and would let the CSM know they had the wrong Ernie. After a while he didn't get the first call anymore.

My drinking and mouth got me taken off as Line NCO and I spent the last half of the tour doing OP duty like many others. Drank out of a good job. Dumbfuck. If you were there you know I wasn't the only one though!!!

Well I must say my opinion of the UN declined in a hurry. You see, if we were on a mission to keep the Greeks and Turks from fighting shouldn't we be allowed to have a loaded magazine on our weapon, and not in our fuckin pocket with orders not to fire unless fired upon. A lot of fuckin' good that would do if you were already dead.

Two things have stuck with me my entire life from Cyprus. Two important things anyway.

The first was being presented my UN Medal from the late Lady Patricia (The Countess Mountbatten of Burma, our Colonel in Chief), while I was on OP duty. That picture is still with my Military display (the cover of the book) all these years later and it also made 75th Anniversary addition of the Patrician, our units Magazine. Even though my name in the picture was soldier, it was me giving her the spiel we had at each OP. It's the picture I usually post on Facebook on our Regimental Birthday. Always will be something I will treasure, and as any Patricia will attest too, Lady Patricia was one of the most respectful people I have met in my life. She loved her troops.

As every OP had a spiel to give to Officers or Dignitaries, I was the one to present it to her, though I am sure she knew them all by heart as she visited any UN Tour or deployment her troops were on. Usually to personally present the UN Peace Keeping medal.

With my troubles and doing so many extra duties, let's just say I had them all memorised.

The thing was, I wasn't to give the spiel, but instead it was supposed to be young Kenny Surridge. It was obvious he hadn't done as many extra's as me and he stumbled the spiel a couple times, where I was the professional for all the wrong reasons, and got my picture of glory in the process. Sometimes crime does pay.

RICHARD (ERNIE) OKRAINEC

Giving the spiel to Lady Patricia-Made My Hometown Paper

There are many stories about how she was with the troops. One example was the time she was being driven around by the late Tim Downing. While pulled into Ledra Palace and escorting her in, some idiot stole the flags off the car. The Flags of a Dignitary and that was bad news for Tim. Even though this was by no means his fault, he could have been in trouble. He was also very pissed off that someone would do this to Lady Patricia. Despite some wanting to blame Tim, she ordered nothing would happen to him and nothing ever did.

She also used to visit us as well back at the Battalion in Winnipeg. We would practise the parade for about a week prior to her arriving. We then would all be formed up for her, ready for the inspection and she would get on the podium, apologise to the Officers, and call us in just to stand around her so we could all hear her. I can't say this enough, as troops, we all loved her.

The other story I still tell to this day was the three day Escape and Evasion exercise we did in the Kyrenia Mountains. This exercise was having Section Commanders lead a section to certain grid points that we had to find via compass and a map while trying to not be caught by the MP's. If caught you were treated as a prisoner of war. The tasks were things like, on the other side of this mountain is a church; what's the name of the church? Then quite a few miles away is a Café; how many windows does it have? There were several points we had to get to each day, on foot with our gear and a compass. Accomplish the tasks while surviving on our own for the three days. Looking back, what an awesome training opportunity. I was the Mcpl and found out I did know how to use a compass, as the places weren't easy to get too, and on foot. Going over small mountains of contour farming of grapes and thorny vines wasn't the fun part though, but a shortcut.

It was hard work and everyone who got the chance likely had their own set of challenges. For me I was glad I got to do it as really this was the first time leading on my own. It helps when you have a good crew though, which I did. Just wish I could remember all the names. Wilky, Gooding, Robideau and others.

Cyprus Escape and Evasion 1982-83

I had heard from some of the earlier patrols that they had slept outside in the cold of the mountains, which certainly wouldn't have been very comfortable at all. So what we did one night was rolled, well walked, into a Turk or Greek Village (can't remember which) and found what could be described as a coffee gathering place. It was a poor village. Of course the people in there didn't speak English and certainly us Turk or Greek. Through it all someone realized we were looking for a barn or something with a roof to sleep. One gentleman got the picture and got us to follow him to his home. He had kind of a second sleeping building of some sort with two or three beds. He offered it to us and we were happy to have beds. What he also did was amazing. He brought my section into his home, his family cooked us supper, gave us homemade wine and we sat around for the evening watching soccer. Half in the bag and no sentries looking for the MP`s. Ha those Meatheads weren't finding us here. And those other poor fuckers slept on the mountain in the cold….ha. We had a long hump to the first checkpoint the next day and had to get underway early. He ensured we were up, cooked us breakfast and sent us on our way. We couldn't thank him enough, but we did leave him $40 Pounds on the bed without telling him, which was around $100 in those days. I found out later that was around a year's wages for him. It was then I found out what it was like to be poor and what doing without was. It made what he did for us even more important. Hope he made good use of the money. Sorry Wilky I don't think I paid you back.... sucker.....I mean invoice me.

I have never forgotten this, realizing in Canada we have it pretty damn good. This was just an act of being a good human to us. That's also what pisses me off when Canadians are bashing our own country, having never really been anywhere, other than a vacation. Really if you don't like it here don't let the door hit your ass on the way out. But that's just me.

And just a finish up to the Escape and Evasion with a neat event that happened on our last day. We had spent the better part of the day off the roads and humping through a ravine which had thick bush for cover, when we came upon a town and we desperately wanted something warm to drink, especially coffee. I was a bit nervous about escaping though, if we had to, seeing it would be difficult, as there was only one road in and one road out of town and we knew the MP's were on our tail. So I set up a sentry at each end of town and we stopped in a coffee place in full gear, weapons and all. There were about eight to ten people in the shop and they were used to the UN being around and weren't too surprised to see us. Well of course not long after, as we were enjoying our hot coffee, suddenly one of the troops came running to let me know the MP's were rolling in. They had jeeps and a truck. It was short notice with no back door and we were basically fucked with nowhere to go. They likely spotted us coming over the mountain and were tracking us knowing we may be in the area. We started to hide behind the tables as there was a big window in the front and it was difficult not to be noticed. We were fucked to say the least.

It was then that the patrons figured out what was going on and they all got up and stood in front of the window, blocking the view from the outside and all waved at the MP's as they slowly drove by. It was awesome. We thanked them and buggered off.

Of course there was a drinking story right after. There were five or six patrols out all over the place. I got back about the same time as Rui Amaral's section and we got into the rum pretty quick waiting for the others and the ride back. The army still had the Old Navy Rum waiting for us in those days and being our rum ration, there was some extra. Being so tired, with not much sleep for three days, well we got drunk pretty quick. Next thing I remember I woke up at the same time as Rui and we were alone in an army van being towed back. Everyone else was gone home in the vans that worked, but they couldn't get us up and chucked us in the van that didn't work. We looked at each other and laughed our asses off. So we got back a few hours later than the rest....but at least it was another great story.

When we were back at the home grounds I was at Ledra Palace, as mentioned earlier. Back then there was no such thing as a regular phone to call home, so we were allocated a certain amount of credits each month to make a call, or we could make a call via Ham Radio for free. Talking via Ham Radio wasn't private at all as everyone in the Ham Radio verse listens to what you say and you have to say "Over" each time you finished your sentence. The other sort of phone system, the one where we were allotted credits, well that could be interesting as well when some of the boys would call home and pass out while talking and their credits kept rolling, which they'd have to pay for later. Thus the reason back then that letters were important, and again the care packages. Though one time my dad made homemade sausage, which he knows is my favorite. Well he and my mom sent me pictures of all the rings he made along with a dried piece of skin in the envelope. Damn Them!! And here I was eating Kebab.

Usually if we were calling home we'd set it up in advance so whomever you were calling would in fact be around. Especially with the time difference, as we were at the other end of the world. A funny story I remember was a Sgt. phoning home to his wife. He had let her know via letter the time and date he'd call. So he kept calling and calling but there wasn't an answer. So the next letter he received, his wife had asked why he hadn't called. She noted she knew he was calling so when she went to visit the neighbour she brought the phone with her and plugged it into their phone jack, but for some reason it didn't work and she never got the call. Remember this was in the day long before cellphones. We laughed our asses off.

We also used to get news from home very slow. Keep in mind a phone was a luxury and there was no internet, but they still managed to live broadcast on the radio the Grey Cup Game. My buddy, the late Frank Leggett, was from the east and I was from the west. He was on duty and couldn't listen to the game and forgot it was on. We got a replay the next day and I bet him $100 Pounds that Edmonton, who I hated, being a Bomber Fan, would beat Toronto, who he was a fan of being from the city. He agreed. Knowing the score I won the bet and didn't tell him for a couple weeks. Too funny and I wouldn't give him the money back.

There were many countries deployed to Cyprus over the years. Some included Australia, Sweden, Finland, Denmark, Iceland, New Zealand, Austria, the UK, Canada, of course, and many others. We'd run into them over time, usually the Swede's or the Brit's. When units collide it usually doesn't always go well, that's the nature of being infantry, but it was the Brits I disliked the most at the time. They had a bad habit of beating up our troops when they were on their own on a night out. I saw the results of a few of the five or six on one shit kicking's that some of the boys had to endure. Many of us certainly were not fans of them at all. We had some big brawls with them as well, including when in Germany.

Throughout the tour there were dozens upon dozens of drinking incidents in Cyprus that affected many of us. Had quite a few buddies who spent their fair share of time in jail. I avoided jail, my jail was the Op's.

There is one awesome story that really blends with my time in Cyprus and my posting to Germany that I just have to tell.

One night, this is in Cyprus, my buddy Al got all liquored up and went to, I believe, the Officers Mess and stole a fake AK47 and held a young officer hostage for a while, just messing with him. Well it certainly scared the shit out of the officer who didn't know the gun was a fake. The officer was pretty messed up after the incident and sent home. I will say I did feel for the young officer though. Al was sent for some brain work, so to speak, and that was the end of him as far as his tour. The shit you do pissed.

Well other than that story, I never thought much about Al as I moved on in my career. Well fast forward to around 1985 and I was walking back late at night from the beer tent to my third story apartment in Germany. As I walked in I saw there was someone passed out face down on my stairs. I rolled him over and it was fuckin' Al. I threw him over my shoulder and brought him to my couch to sleep a bit more comfortably.

When he got up in the morning, he looked at me with bloodshot eyes, as we hadn't seen each other in about three years, and with a big grin says, "Holy Christ Ernie, I was wondering where the fuck I was." We laughed our asses off.

Ledra Palace was quite a big place which also had the Junior Ranks, a Mess Hall, along with the Senior NCO's and Officers Mess included. We spent a lot of time in our own mess areas, but it wasn't always drinking. We played lots of games and became good at whatever the game was. There was everything from the Euchre and Crib Tournaments, to Ping Pong, Foosball, and Darts. You got even better if you had extras and had long days of Duty NCO in there and just played the games. That's how many people also became so good at pool. There was also a movie room which played two or three movies through the days and nights, as everyone was on shift work, and a canteen that would cook the late night munchies when the Kitchen was closed. The place had everything you needed.

While we were on tour we knew we were getting posted to Germany in a couple years, so many of us took our two week vacation there during the tour. They had kind of a leave center on the Base in Lahr, Germany and we moved around from there. When I took my vacation, the trip included three is us including Wild Bill. Those who remember Bill would know wild is a mild term once drinks were added.

Well the three of us bought a nine day First Class train pass so we could get on and off any train and ensured we had a place to sleep or pass out. The train system in Europe is awesome.

Well, what can I say, it was a shit show from the start as we bought the entire liquor cart when it went by a half an hour into our first ride, and that was breakfast. Over the couple of weeks we lost Wild Bill a couple times but he always showed up a couple days later. If you knew Bill you would also know losing him wasn't a shock, and also that when he was hammered, many times you didn't mind losing him for a while. Lost him on the train once, but found him when we heard a loud slap as he was trying to pick up a lady. He was a crazy man, but fun.

We were up somewhere in Northern Germany and asking how to get back to Lahr. They didn't understand where Lahr was but said, "Up here Lahr is called Chur." "Well ok, then how do we get there?" They told us and we took their directions and got on the train, only to find out that the Chur they were talking about was in Czech Republic, and in those days we weren't allowed there. Once we saw the sign we were getting close to Czechoslovakia we managed to get off about ten minutes before the border and laughed our asses off looking for a bar.

Well, I'd like to say we went to all the Museums and Historical sites all around the country during the two weeks, but I'll note Reeperbahn and leave it there.

We did get to celebrate New Year's at some large hotel we rented a room in. Think it was in Munich. When we got into our room there was a liquor fridge. It was my first ever liquor fridge in a hotel and we all thought it was pretty cool to be included with the room. I mean how fuckin' awesome is that? Think about that journey. I was twenty by then, in a hotel for New Years with free booze, and a tenth floor balcony. We invited a bunch of Germans to party with us, shooting fireworks from the balcony like everyone else, and said, "Help yourself to our free booze." Great time was had by all.

Well something happened at checkout, as we found out we needed an additional $800 Deutsche Marks for the booze we drank. Dumbfucks. We laughed our asses off. We had just enough money to pay it off.

So now we are halfway through our holiday and almost broke. The next adventure was getting money. There were no computers or cell phones back then. So the adventure was using the train pass to find a TD Bank so we could get some money wired. The TD was across the street from the base in Winnipeg, so most of us dealt there. We found there was one in Stuttgart and we hopped the train to get there. Couple nights and cabs later we found it. It was opening and the one in Canada was closing. The German Banker called there, the Banker back home spoke with us on the phone to confirm, well I shouldn't say us as it was me and my money, and I got him to wire an emergency $2,000, which was about $5,000 Deutsche Marks. He laughed. The money got there next day and when we got it I had one Canadian dime left, which I gave to a beggar.

Well rolling in that much cash would have lasted lesser men, but we made sure we spent every last fuckin' nickle of that money in about four or five days. I remember we got back to Lahr and were getting ready, in the bar, to go back to Cyprus and spending the last of the money on a round of drinks for a bunch of buddies. So of course I was walking back to the table with a full tray of drinks, tripped and dumped all the drinks on the table. That's how the holiday ended. Rui looked up and down at all the spilled drinks and we laughed our asses off. I don't remember if my travelling partners ever paid me back, but no matter, it was an adventure.

The rest of the Cyprus Tour was uneventful as far as I remember and I had some good Senior NCO's helping me get back on track, which I certainly appreciated later. It wasn't the smoothest transition to Mcpl for sure, but I lived to tell a few stories about it.

In the war zone of the Green Line there were many wild cats and dogs for sure. When troops walked or drove around, more often than not, we likely carried a puppy pounder, a pick ax handle, with us. We all knew you just didn't mess with them, as they were not tame puppies or cats. The cats were fuckin' crazy. They certainly were not pets. We had a guy in the Battalion who was there on a previous tour who caught something from one of the cats, from which he lost all of the hair on his body. You just didn't pet them, even if you found a friendly one.

In the more open areas the dogs would be in packs. Sometimes they would chase the jeep. You'd go fast enough until they were close, hammer on the breaks, and a couple would run into the jeep and you'd fuck off praying you didn't stall the jeep. In Ledra Palace and all over the OP's there were cats around. I remember playing ping pong in Ledra Palace and a ceiling tile came crashing down on the table with a cat on it. It was cruising through the ceiling. Well the cat went nuts trying to get out. They were vicious. Heard also a cook had one cornered in the kitchen and it tried to attack him.

We carried mace as well on the Op's. One day when I was up on OP Maple 42, which was the tower, I believe, and pretty high up. About five or six floors maybe. Also believe that was the OP where the Canadian soldier was killed in the 70's. Anyway this Op was quite high. We used to spray the wild cats with mace from up there and they'd be quite pissed off and try to climb the wall of the tower to get us. They were wicked.

We sure partied when we had the opportunity for sure. Some more than others. After Jessie died I suppose it's true what we were told. In our job we partied when we had the chance as you just never knew when your last day may be. I don't know, it's hard to explain. After Bosnia and Afghanistan and seeing so much loss, it was their last day. As I get older there are way too many leaving us, but we still honor all of them with pictures and memories on Facebook. It's always amazing how much respect is given from the brotherhood of every generation when that fateful picture is posted of another loss of someone. Civvies don't get that like we do.

That moment of drifting from Cyprus was brought to you from the mind of Ernie Okrainec; now back to Cyprus you idiot and get off the rum.

A Nice Trip Down Memory Lane

OP life could be pretty boring for sure, but it was better than being at the front gate of Ledra Palace where you had to deal with every Dignitary who came and went. The best part was when they decided we should live on the line where the OP's were. It got us away from all the eyes at Ledra Palace. So for much of the second half of the tour I got to live out there and it was awesome, compared to Ledra Palace. We had great troops with us. Who would have thought living in a rougher environment would be better than having a room of your own. We made the best of it and along the way we laughed our asses off. We didn't get into much trouble out on the line. We just did our job without everyone around telling us how to do it.

If anyone took the time to get around Cyprus, it really is a tourist place with great beaches. If we went to the leave centre in Larnaca or Limassol the troops were looked after with an apartment room with some food, though we never ate in the room, we ate at the bar or restaurants, and the room had beer fridge. Damn, it wasn't stalked with free liquor. It was just a place to get away when we had two or three days off. I didn't take advantage of it until later in the tour. Early on I spent too much time downtown in Nicosia coming home to too many eyes.

The winter tour certainly wasn't as hot as the summer tour for sure. It wrapped up in March of 1983 and then it was back to Winnipeg.

Later the two sides reconciled their differences. I believe, in part, there was a very large earthquake in one of either Turkey or Greece and one helped the other and solved some issues. The Cyprus Tour ended in the 90's.

CHAPTER 6
Flyover-Germany-Fall 1983

Once we were back in Canada we were back in training schedules and garrison life again. Along the way I got the Machine Gun Course, the Sigs Course, Driver Wheel, Driver Track and others I can't remember, but pretty much most everyone took the various courses when we were in training cycles. One of the best things I ever saw was a night fire exercise on the machine gun course. The 50 cal ammo belts had every fourth round, I think, as a tracer round, meaning you could see the red tipped round blazing towards your target. So when there were around 20 x 50 cal machine guns rolling in the pitch black it was a sight to see all those red rounds hitting a target at a high rate of speed. Some of us would try and rig the belt to be mostly tracer rounds only. When you were done shooting the barrel of the gun was glowing red hot. It was pretty damn cool to see.

Now imagine 20 guns of tracers going at the same time

Once back in Canada my job was in Admin (Administration) Company as a Signals NCO. This was a pretty decent job as I worked most of the time on my own and didn't really have to answer to anyone most days. While I was there I was offered the opportunity to be attached back with a rifle company, can't remember which but the late CSM Mackay was in charge, to be part of the flyover Company heading to Germany for six to eight weeks. Well to say the least I jumped at that chance pretty fuckin quick.

Remember when I said never to volunteer, well that wasn't always the case and this was Germany.

It was also my first look at the Baden Base that we were getting posted to the following year.

Well as professional troopers and in typical soldier fashion the first night in Germany was a huge go out and party night. Sounds familiar I suppose. Can't remember exactly what and where the party was, and being in Germany it really could have been anywhere. I do remember getting up in the morning, still half in the bag, and cutting myself shaving pretty badly. Blood was so thin that the bleeding wouldn't stop, so I had to go on parade with a gob of toilet paper attached to my face. Pretty much all of us had partied and were still half cut and we were expecting some grief for sure. Well that was until the CSM called the parade to attention, did an about face to the Major and almost fell over. And the Major was just as bad. So problem solved and no inspection required.

Funny how I can remember the fun shit but don't recall much about the exercise, other than we were in the field a lot, well pretty much the entire time, and were also on trains for many hours as that was how we got around. When not on trains we drove the tracks down any of the roads civilian traffic was on. Also, in our life we rolled from one exercise to the next and after a while they start to all be the same shit, different weather, different month, when is End Ex and where's my field pay.

The exercise and training was pretty much the same we would do over the four years we would spend in Germany, very large Brigade Level, living in the field, attached with other members of the Forces and so on. You'd also be on some long road moves for sure. We all learned to live in the back of a track with six to ten of us bouncing around trying to get comfortable. The training in Germany, for the most part, was always pretty good. Very much different than what we were used to in Canada, as we were actually in towns throughout countryside. Sometimes in someone's back yard. They almost always welcomed you.

So when we were in the field we worked, sometimes our ass off, no eight to five shift, just long hours, including many a night in any kind of weather standing in the trenches we dug. Then, when we didn't work sometimes we went hard and didn't waste the day. This was even better if we happened to be near a town. Not much to do when we were deep in the bush with time off, other than confirming if bears actually shit in the woods. There wasn't such a thing as weekends or days off, just some downtime in between. It really depended where we were. Sometimes that would be our life for weeks or months on end.

Home was where you parked

We also had field pay I mentioned. This was money we accumulated each day for the amount of time spent in the field from which they would pay us at the end of the exercise. I think it was around $8.00 a day. The pay usually came shortly after the glorious words, "End Ex." (The end of the exercise when we all got word over the radio that the Exercise was over and we knew we were finally done) and most of us spent that money wherever we were, like a reward. So after six weeks of next to no days off, it was then, "Here's your $360.00, see ya in the morning." Converted to the German Deutsche Mark it was around $700DM. And let's face it, we could do a lot in one night with those kinds for funds. And.....we did.

I used to laugh as some of the guys who didn't tell their wives about field pay, then we'd bring it up at a party at their place and the shit would hit the fan. My thought, even though I wasn't married at the time, was I'm the fucking one living the dream in the field and that money will be 100% invested into creature comforts at the appropriate time. It's just sometimes those creature comforts included liquor.

So now it's End Ex, and we are getting our field pay and the Sgt. says, "Alright boys don't get too pissed!!" Well that sounded like a challenge to us. Challenge accepted.

Well......naturally that didn't go as planned. We were in a field at the time living in our bivy area and close to a small town and that amount of money, over $700 DM's, was getting burnt. (The bivouac was the area we camped out in and was moved various times throughout the exercise. We were never in the same place very long and moved around a lot.) A few of us headed out and this one private was hounding me and wanted to hang around, but we didn't want him around. He wasn't a popular guy and was getting on my nerves for the better part of six weeks and certainly we weren't buddies. After about an hour of following me around and pestering me I was at the end of my rope and I turned around and drifted him in the chops. He went down and I told him to fuck off and not follow us around anymore. He didn't and more on that later but not a smart move Mcpl Okrainec. Dumbfuck

Well the whole company had a hoot wherever it was that they ended up. As the troops started to stagger in, well, it was kind of like the walking dead, in green. Last thing of the night before that I remember was trying to find my way back to the bivy. I could hear the tracks running but couldn't find them. I was walking in a field, was tired, so sat down for a rest and woke up in the morning in a dewy frosted swath and I was the farmers next round, freezing my ass off.

I stumbled back to the bivy, now that I could see with sunrise upon us, and pretty much everyone looked like they came from under a rock. One brother, Mike Trenholm who has since passed, even beat up a car, that he didn't remember doing, but kind of remembered, and paid for the car later, while taking responsibility. It was ugly out for sure. Checked my wallet. Well that didn't go well. We looked around and laughed our asses off. What a fuckin shit show.

So this guy I popped in the mouth, well turns out he reported that I beat the shit out of him. So guess who was hungover and in front of the hungover CSM.

"Welcome back Okrainec, where have we seen this movie before?"

I had seen him several times in Cyprus, so we could say we knew each other quite well. Other than the fact when I saw him in Cyprus, it wasn't to have a drink, but instead I was standing at attention getting chewed out. He was an awesome CSM and I enjoyed working with him.

"Good seeing you as well CSM."

He let me give my full version of events and also let me demonstrate how this guy was annoying me, other than punching him of course, and he said,

"You know you are not supposed to punch Privates in the mouth even if that's what's required, right Mcpl?"

"Sure do CSM. Dumbfuck thing to do but I'd had enough."

Well turns out this tool jumped off a track to try and hurt himself more and basically beat himself up so I'd get in trouble. But I had buddies who saw that didn't happen the way he reported the incident.

So now we are back on base, and I'm wondering what's up, as we are all called on parade. Of course I am fully expecting my punishment. Well the Sgt., who was my Sgt. Ed Haines, was going down the ranks doing an inspection and stops in front of this guy, found something wrong during the inspection, which of course could always happen, and that he was being put up on charges. In the end nothing happened to me. Ok, maybe not Dumbfuck.

Though I was sure I wasn't shooting up any promotion ranks, I had no complaints how that turned out. But I looked in my wallet again....Where the fuck did my field pay go?

I think this story was returning back to Canada, but may be a different time, but the story happened none the less.

When troops flew Service Air (Armed Forces Air) there of course was the saying, "Time to spare, fly service air," because usually there was much waiting for long periods of time for the flight, which never seemed to be on time. The price was right though, free. Well this time it was delayed thirty six hours or so. Our Officers made us stay in the terminal as they figured if we got out we'd get pissed. Geez... no faith. So now we are finally ready to go and they said there were issues with the gear packed in the bottom of the plane and that it wasn't balanced properly to leave. Meaning we'd have to wait even longer. Our Major was annoyed and got us out of the terminal onto the tarmac. We then unloaded the plane and repacked it properly and the plane balance turned out fine. The Air Force guys weren't happy but we were Infantry and didn't like them anyway. After that we were finally on our way, after almost two days in a terminal. People wonder why we can sleep anywhere.

From the winter of 1983 to the spring of 1984 it was more or less all preparations for our upcoming four year posting to Germany. Oh of course there was still time spent in the woods and general training. There always was. There were also a lot of weddings before, including myself and many buddies. Over the long haul there sure are not many still together from those younger days, including me, but there were some fun times as well.

The Battalion sent us off from Canada in style for sure. From the Freedom of the City Marches in downtown Winnipeg to the Gala Events in the old Arena, which were a sight to see, it was a first class farewell to the City of Winnipeg.

Without a doubt though the most fun was something called the Better Ole on our Base. This was a massive bar set up in one of the large buildings on the base which was decorated as bunkers, trenches and filled with sandbags. It was also open twenty four hours a day and held many events and parties over the week. Of course I was part of the shiftwork crew working in the Better Ole building. The same Sgt. from Cyprus was in charge and of course I got saddled with all the Midnight to eight in the morning shifts as he didn't want to miss anything, which both sucked and was awesome. Had a lot of fun and to say the least, saw some very interesting things through the night. Even the stories from the shacks would have blushed.

It was so much fun, but had to come to an end, maybe for our livers sake, and now it was packing up and heading for an opportunity of a lifetime. West Germany.

CHAPTER 7
CFB Baden-Sollegen-West Germany-1984-88

Yes I had the opportunity to be in Europe when there still was an East and West Germany, actually it was the reason we were there. The Cold War. Though coming back in 1988 I missed witnessing the Berlin Wall coming down by about a year. That would have been a sight to see, as we weren't allowed in any of those areas or countries during our stay in Europe. Also it would have been awesome to see the freedom of the people coming from East Germany after all those years of being separated, or seeing families reunited after many decades.

I couldn't think of a better place to essentially grow up. We did lots of cool training all over the place from which I'll thumbnail some stories I remember. And while we were away a lot, you know we took advantage of our time off for sure. We all didn't just party, we travelled a lot during our time off. We were ten minutes from the Rhine River and France. Anyone could see three countries every trip, Austria, Switzerland, France, Italy, Spain, England, Holland, Belgium, they were all within distance, so we took advantage and travelled. I also travelled as a result of sports and being I am a history guy, there was plenty to see in Europe. My hometown in Canada was celebrating its 100th birthday while I was in Germany. The town I was living in while posted was celebrating its $1,100^{th}$. This is why Europeans still refer to us as being from the new world. And I mean really, who could forget Oktoberfest, Beer Tents. Tiff's or Benny's Balloon Bar and many other establishments. There was something at every turn.

Unfortunately it wasn't always a party. We talk that way as that's the memories we want to remember, the good times to try and forget the bad. I had a Civvy buddy ask why we partied so hard. Said it's because we just never knew when it would be our last one. He noted that's what his grandfather said as well from WWII, but they were in a whole other situation than I was. This was the Cold War.

We were bugged out a lot, which meant you'd get a call, usually in the middle of the night, to get into the base with all our gear and pack up and be ready to be deployed. Sometimes it was just a drill to see how quick we'd get in, other times it was off on the train, with no notice, and then be gone sometimes six to eight weeks. That's why we were always packed and ready to go. There was no such thing as weekends or holidays when we were in the field. We were in the field and this was no holiday. This life was also certainly hard on family life as troops just could be up and gone with little or no notice.

Well crap, as I get started on my adventures, I likely could write a novel just about Germany. There are stories and adventures from all over Europe, as really I grew up there in my twenty two to twenty six year old days. When I was posted to Baden I didn't want to come back to Canada for any holiday, and didn't. I travelled Europe instead. I only ended up back in Canada for courses or sports. Back to Edmonton to get my wings on the Jump Course, back to Gagetown for Advance Comms (Advance Communications), to Ottawa and Edmonton for Broomball and think that was it. I had many many friends and family come to visit. Each visit was fun at the time for sure and gave us excuses to travel and party even more. More importantly, it gave them an excuse for a European holiday and many of them took advantage of that.

I certainly won't be able to write and tell all the stories in a chronological order, so I will just tell the stories of the journey and events along the way.

I arrived on July 1 and thought there would be some form of a Canada Day Celebration, instead everything was just green. Baden was also much larger than Kapyong Barracks for sure and we were attached with many of the other trades needed on the base. Mostly, when we first arrived, the Air Force and other trades were scared of us, like we were going to bite their babies or something. Over time we all got to know many of them and made some good friends. For many of us, it was also our first time being posted on the same base as the other forces. Usually the Infantry had their own base. After being essentially segregated on our own for so long, integrating with the other units was interesting at times.

My home was a popular gathering spot over the years, on the third floor of the Sparkasse Bank in Hugelsheim, just outside of the base. It was a couple kilometers from the base, down the street from the main hangout bar, Tiffs, down the other way of the street from the towns Beer Tent, a couple of doors down from my landlords Gasthaus (Their awesome Restaurants), right close to the liquor store, and all liquor and goods for us were duty free. Forty ounce bottles were $3-5 DM's per bottle, German Beer was awesome, and we also were issued a liquor ration card to use each month. Hell, even McDonalds had Beer Machines. It was just a much different culture than Canada. Between a couple, we were only allowed 8 x 40 ounce bottles per month (If I remember correctly, it could have been four) and all the beer or wine we wanted. Oh it was the fucking torture for sure. It was a stressful situation and I was filing a complaint about all the liquor opportunities but couldn't find any additional witnesses to further my complaint so I was forced to power through the best I could.

You'll also now understand why it was not a complete shock to find Al on my stairs. We were a hangout or passout spot like the rest in the building. Reg Eddy, Johnny Juniper, Kevin Torfasson, Tony & Dee Dee. It was a really fun crew.

At first when we arrived we couldn't get beers off-sale on Sunday, other than a restaurant, but we could phone the base pizza joint and order a small fries and 48 Killer Heineken (tall boys) and they would deliver. Man life sucked.

But other than that we didn't drink much. Where the fuck did my field pay go?

We were very much the, "I can't make it back to base and need a place to passout for three days or so," like many others who lived in Hugey or any of the other towns around the Base.

Sure were some good times. We laughed our asses off.

They always sent news home to the local paper

As soldiers though, we were also gone a lot, so we took advantage of the time we had off. In my fourth year in Germany I was away on various training and courses for eight months. Such was our life and also hard on the family life for sure. Which is why we as soldiers, are so close. We were all away and at times only had each other. So we watched each other's backs.

Being at the other end of the world also was hard on the family back home as well. A phone was still somewhat of a luxury, though we all had one, but to phone back to Canada was very expensive. So keeping in touch wasn't easy. The letters were so important back then.

For those with kids I can't imagine all the growing up things they missed over the years when they were deployed somewhere. Or how difficult it was for their kids when they were posted to various bases and had to pack up and move on a regular basis and have to make new friends. The older kids were called Base Brats and had to live the sometimes constant moving around from Base to Base. It wasn't easy for them either. This is the same for most of the Armed Forces throughout Canada.

During the tour my Grandfather passed away and I felt helpless somewhat. I asked my 2 I/C Captain if I could go back for the funeral and was told no he couldn't make the arrangements. I believe he just didn't want to make the arrangements, as not long after I noticed another Officer had lost someone back in Canada and got to go back. Such was the challenges we lived.

I really can't get too far into stories about Germany without getting to life with an Autobahn. We all quickly got used to driving fast, all the time. Not long after getting there we got an Audi. They were common just like the BMW's, Mercedes, Peugeots, Porches, you name it. All built to go fast. We certainly got to places a lot quicker. During my tour I did see one Lamborghini, but it wasn't for very long as he passed me in a blink of an eye and was gone, while I was doing 180 Kms.

However, if you were under twenty five years old you paid dearly for insurance. It was based on your age and the horse power of the vehicle. I believe I paid $2,500 DM's per year for insurance on the Audi. At the end of the tour I had bought a VW Rabbit to try and slow down a bit in preparation to return to Canada, and by then I was twenty five, so my insurance dropped to around $180 DM's per year. That's why not many young Germans had their own vehicles, and we'd see many mopeds, as it was too expensive to own a vehicle.

Not long after arriving in Germany we were off to Fall Ex for eight weeks. This was the same Ex I did for flyover the year prior. I was back in a rifle company at that time.

So it was back in the field and certainly we made a big mistake. Now I can't remember if it was the first Exercise, but it definitely happened, as I was part of the awful journey. We were at a Brit Base and what we did was fill all of our water containers from the wash racks and headed out for the exercise. The wash racks was the area we all cleaned the mud off the vehicles. Well it turned out the water in the wash racks was contaminated and not for drinking, just washing the tracks and vehicles. Well nobody told us that. All of us, and I mean fucking all, got the shits. I mean it was the thought you had a little fart and shit yourself shits.

There were so many bad shit stories. Once, as we were just heading out on patrol one guy in my Section says, "Mcpl I have to run back to the shacks. I just shit myself going over that bump."

We all had a story like that. Shit yourself through the night. It was fucking awful. But as soldiers we carried on for a day or two and didn't miss any training. It wasn't very fun trying to dig a trench squeezing your cheeks as tight as you could, but we did it anyway, just a whole lot slower.

After some time pushing through the best we could the CSM came by to each area, called us all troopers, and eventually they cancelled a portion of the exercise. They also had to emergency drop something like 15,000 rolls of toilet paper. We were put on a soup ration, while those who weren't sick got to eat meat.....in front of us.... Fuckers.

Troops would come out of the shitter with a big "YAHOO" when they had that first solid shit and they knew they would be able to eat the solid food again. We laughed our asses off, well not the usual laugh the ass off, as we didn't want to shit ourselves. Goodbye several pairs of underwear, I enjoyed our moments together.

Exercises were very different in Germany, compared to Canada, as more often than not we were in a town, someone's yard or a field right next to a town. If we were at a Parkplatz (Parking Lot) likely there was an opportunity to get a shower at some Rec Centre.

One good thing for sure was being that close to town we'd rarely eat rations. This was even better because the rations in those days sucked, very much. Some of this food was back to the Vietnam War Era. If in town troops got over to the bakery for fresh bread and sandwich meat and gave the rations away to the kids so it at least looked like we were eating them. No one wanted the CO or some Senior Officer to come by and see there was still boxes upon boxes of rations unopened, as good things usually get taken away by those who were jealous they didn't have them. We certainly didn't want some order coming down that we would only be allowed to eat rations.

It would be funny though, as sometimes we'd be in the middle of the Black Forrest, dug in, sitting in some trench (it was warm so I didn't have to wiggle my toes) and doing sentry duty, when we'd hear a muffler of some sort coming down the trail. Sometimes it would be a little truck or a motorbike, and offering us bread and sandwich meat to buy. Even they knew where we were. Field pay went to other things besides liquor.

Why the hell eat rations

We were all over the country so it made sense they would take advantage. No one would ever treat them bad for sure.

See I spent field pay on some good things as well. Creature comforts.

Just as an aside, one group that was also everywhere we went was the Sally Ann. They were small supply locations which provided books, snacks, knives and all kinds of various items in whatever shop they had set up. Cyprus, Germany and many other places in between. They were a breath of fresh air for us and I know I always appreciated when they were around. They helped take your mind off things. They are the ones who got me into reading to pass time, and I had quite the knife collection over the years. For me the knives had to always have the toothpick. The plastic toothpick was important as it lasted forever and I always didn't have a chance to brush my teeth. That's what gum in our rations was used for.

This latest off topic journey was again brought to you by Ernie Okrainec. Now back on topic over in Germany dipshit.

During my time in Germany I was in a Rifle Company, Admin (Administration) Company and Sigs (Signals). So in the beginning, I lived the rough dig a trench life and the last half I didn't. I certainly enjoyed the second half of the tour much more than the first, as far as being in the field. In that last half, I drove a 2 ½ ton Truck and later the MLVW (Medium Logistics Vehicle Wheeled which was about the same size just newer) and slept in the back of that very comfortably off the ground. Ate at many restaurants and sentry duty was a tad more laid back in A Ech (at the rear with the rest of supply group). I didn't complain. The last year I was Battalion Sigs Stores so was kind of the CQ (Company Quartermaster) for Sigs and supplied all Radio's, Equipment and Accessories for the Battalion.

Where's my field pay

I certainly didn't forget some of the days in the beginning being a Mcpl in a Rifle Section and having the all night State 2 and 3 marches (Gas Drills. State 3 included the Gas Suit and Gas Masks, State 2 was just the Gas Suit), sometimes doing patrols through the night in the rain. It really sucked being wet and cold, but everyone was the same so you sucked it up. Nor did I miss the fun times trying to dig trenches in rock or through roots. Ya that was fun. Swing, ding, sparks, fuck, swing, ding, sparks, fuck. Not the damn camping that Recruiter told me about.

Being Infantry we learned we could sleep anywhere, in any position, and our sleep would be based on how long we had. Whether it be against a tree, on rocks, in a ditch, in the back of the APC's...anywhere. I can still catnap to this day. Just sometimes being old, the evening catnap rolls in and around three hours.

You didn't waste 5-minutes if you needed a nappy

The main exercises were located in Hohenfels and Sennelager, but the best was in Hammelburg where we did fighting in a built up area training. The town was used just for this purpose. Fighting in a town, door to door and getting to break stuff and do booby-traps. I went there once with a Rifle Company and did the attacking of the town, where there would be many casualties in real battle, and another time with Sigs, and Rui, from which we were the enemy force and lived in the town and did the training most days as various groups attacked us.

OK whose turn is it to lay on the wire

Kicking in doors, scaling walls three stories up, busting through roofs, building to building clearing, I got to do it all like most everyone else who was there and the training was awesome. They told us when we were through the training we aged the town about two years. We were all into it for sure. Also learned in a hurry it's ugly warfare and there would be many casualties from the attacking side as the enemy can hide pretty darn good in rubble or buildings. We all got very creative in developing hiding spots and booby traps.

RICHARD (ERNIE) OKRAINEC

All Clear

When I was there the first time with a Rifle Company we were crawling through a culvert as a Section. So there were seven or eight of us crawling through the culvert and a Sgt. thought it would be funny throwing an orange smoke grenade into the culvert to see if we could crawl through while not being able to see, and also breathing in the all that fucking smoke. Well wasn't that a good fucking idea. The guy in front of me, Mike, was a major claustrophobic and panicked once this happened. He wouldn't keep crawling forward and tried to back up and we were all stuck in there for about ten to fifteen minutes until we managed to get out. I remember pissing orange for a few days after that. Ya I bet that was really great for my body and lungs.

As mentioned while I was with Sigs, I was kind of the CQ and went and got all the supplies and meals for the boys most days. I also organized a big BBQ Steak Supper for the troops, as there were twenty five or thirty of us living in the town, while the rest of the Battalion lived at the base. Rui, Billy, Mike, Frenchy, Steve, Clay, and so many others used Sigs Stores as the nightly debrief with many beers, thus not much sleep for me, as that was where my bedroom was. Of course I had to take part in the debrief, no matter how tired.

I do remember a crazy night of fart lighting. Much gas from the terrific food we usually ate mixed with much liquor leads to an evening of fart lighting. Billy would call it out, lights off, lighter ready, fart out, burst of flames and we'd laugh are asses off. If you remember Rui's laugh you'd laugh harder. Crack another beer and wait and this went on for a couple of hours. The next day a few of us had singe marks on our pants. We laughed our asses off. Well now a days I am pretty sure I wouldn't be doing that game in my office.

The training there was awesome. The days went fast and I still see many pictures of that training posted on Facebook from the many troops who took part. Just of course, I don't have too many of them.

The other training that was right up there was the Adventure Training that included the all-day climb up the mountain to Berchtesgaden and Hitler's Eagle's Nest. Historical part aside, the view was awe inspiring. We were above the clouds looking down into the valley. It was easy to see why the allies couldn't take the place out as it was difficult to get to, protected and hard to attack. It was located on the corner of a mountain. The story notes the gold elevators were made from the teeth of the Jews, but I don't know that as an actual fact. It wouldn't be a surprise if it was true for sure. The Nazi's were evil.

Holy crap, are we there yet

The entire time getting up the mountain was a bag drag and took the better part of the day, but more than worth it. It was a few miles just to the starting base point before we started climbing up. We all found out what they meant when the air gets thin the higher you climb. We all pooped out a lot quicker and it was tougher to breathe. When we were getting ready to head back down we used a road, so that part was easier than climbing the mountain. The issue though was our toes were banging off the front of our boots during the decent and it started to hurt after a while. So a few of us decided to run down the six to eight miles because it hurt less and of course had some beers at a restaurant until the rest of the troops got down. Was really an overall hump of a day, but man was it worth it.

Getting there

It was worth the hump

During this training we also did some rafting in those big ten to twelve man rafts which turned into its own adventure. The night before our go of the river training there were big rainstorms and the water from the mountains filled the rivers more which meant the water was moving pretty hard compared to the day before. Yee-fuckin-haw. Good luck trying to steer them when they became half full of water with the Sgt. yelling at you to steer better. Ya that wasn't happening. We were going where the current was taking us. We had to duck to get under one bridge, and of course missed the support pillars on the way through. One of the rafts in front of us wasn't so lucky and hit the pillar nose first, it bent in half with the raft being air, and shot about six of them in the air for a splashdown. We all had life jackets so they were safe, but of course on our way by those in the water we laughed our asses off yelling, "See ya at the finish line." That was a ride.

We also did repelling in the mountains with a mix of adventure training at the local bars when we had the night off. It truly was some of the best training and fun in all my exercises throughout my time in the army.

The majority of the training in and around Germany, if you weren't lucky enough to have your own wheeled vehicle, would be spent on trains. Trains moving troops and equipment around were the lowest priority of the train system, even behind livestock, and sometimes we'd be on them for a couple days. Of course we'd pass the time playing euchre or crib. There wasn't much for hand held video games in those days, but they started to come out later in the tour. I got into reading as well during those downtime periods. Started with the Max Bolin books, went to Steven King and haven't looked back, as I read a lot now a days. As soldiers, there was so much hurry up and wait moments that we always found ways to pass time. That's where so many stories are told, and also how we got to know our brothers.

When we were away at another base and were actually living in a barracks it was Board games to pass time. For us it was massive games of Risk, which evolved to Ultimatum. We had many laughs and beers in those long games. Some were halted until the next day when training was scheduled and completed when we came back, and when the game was over, there would be a line of people waiting to start another one. It was the best of times.

I mentioned earlier sometimes there were fights. Well sometimes as well there were brawls. All of us somewhere during our career were involved or saw one and, well, you did your part. It was also at some of these bases that we would be working with the Brits and for the most part we didn't like them and they didn't like us. Many of us, including myself, had held a grudge from Cyprus when they used to gang up on the troops as I mentioned earlier, but being Infantry most other units were rivals, and they were no different. Just at that time they were the biggest rivals. This likely was a result of us training on their bases quite a bit.

One night, I think I was with Charlie Company, we were having a Company Smoker (Steak Night and Drinks) after some training on one of the British Bases. The night was going fine enough, but then some Brits crashed the party. We didn't care too much that they were there, until they started causing shit and looking for trouble. Pouring beer down guys pants, starting arguments, just being dicks in general. Well after a while the boys, including me, just had enough. We started to take it all outside and our Major was trying to calm things down. He was speaking to one of the Brits telling him to just walk away and go somewhere else, but the Brit took a swing at him. Well Emerson Lowry was having none of that, and none of us would let someone from another unit just take a swing at one of our brothers. Well Emerson levelled the Brit in the face, broke his hand doing so, and down went the Brit. The Major said, "Fuck it, C Company attack!!!" so….we attacked. Christ there must have been sixty to eighty troops in total in a full out brawl. There were more of us PPCLI gang, as it was them crashing our party, and I'll just say it didn't go well for those Brits as they were shit kicked. Guess they found out what it was like being outnumbered.

As we were on a Brit Base, a bus full of Red Caps (The British MP's) rolled in to stop the brawl. It was funny as the bus pulled up, they saw how many people were going at it, knew they were massively outnumbered, and likely said, "Fuck that I'm not going in there," and they turned the bus around and drove away. I do know our Major got in trouble for telling us to attack, but sometimes you just defended your honor and the boys. We attacked.

There weren't always fights, but they weren't uncommon either. Sometimes happens when liquor gets involved. I was at another, smaller brawl which I still chuckle about. I believe we were in another bar which also had another one of the PPCLI Battalions. After a while a fight started and a few of the boys were involved. Well, one of my buddies, who may have watched too many movies, decided he would pick up a table and was holding it over his head ready to do damage I suppose. Yup, may have seemed like a good idea at the time, until one of the guys walked up to him with the table above his head and swift kicked him in the nuts. I'll never forget watching him slowly going down, then collapsing on the floor with the table on top of him and I just saw him lying on the floor under a table with his legs sticking out. Well that didn't go as planned. I laughed my ass off. He was ok, but a funny sight to see.

Russ Buckle doing what he did best

We also sang a lot. Every Company or Platoon had someone who played the guitar and sang, or we just sang as a group. This included the late Russ Buckle, plus Kenny Surridge, Fred Hayne and so many others. Even had laughs with Blue Hiway in Germany, a band some of the boys put together with Fred Hayne, Ed Dagenais, Jeff Conroy, Norm Green and Ron Allison. The rest of the crew had Frank Leggett doing the sound, me the lights and Boyd Brandson setting off the explosives during the wrong song. Man had fun stories from those nights. Even more fun as some of this gang were/are my best friends.

Blue Hiway in action

Lights and sound

A great band who gave us great times

Well even something as innocent as singing sometimes lead to issues, when drinks were involved. It also makes sense that of course I was involved somehow.

It was at one of these bases and was one of those nights out and having some drinks. Usually we didn't venture to far and stuck close to the base as we knew we'd shortly be heading out again for training early the next day. During these times it was whatever bar was set up on the base. We were all on a night off and of course closed the bar. I know that's a shock, but really. So on our way back we stopped in the community whizzer to have a final piss and started singing, like many soldiers do, especially while or after drinking. So while this was happening, a WO (Warrant Officer) walked in and started singing and drinking with us. He was in the same state as the rest of us. After a few rounds of songs he asked if we wanted more beer, as he was a CQ and could oblige us.

I didn't say we were good singers but we tried

Well that sounded like a challenge and we accepted. It's funny how things start off innocently enough.

Well we carried on singing there until two or three in the morning and my buddy was leaning against a sink and it accidently broke off. We turned off the water and decided not much could be done that night and that we would report it in the morning. We were not interested in waking someone up this late, and in the bag to boot. This was likely the better option than waking up someone who just wouldn't be happy.

As we were heading back to the shacks the WO was having none of that and wanted it reported right now. He was a good enough guy, just pissed like the rest of us. Well as I was walking in the shacks I noticed he had my other drunken buddy Ron at attention and was chewing him out telling him the incident would be reported right now. Once I saw this taking place I stormed back there and picked up the WO by the collar, shook him around for a bit and said, "You get the fuck to bed right fuckin now," and chucked him down on the ground. Dumbfuck....Really Really Dumbfuck. Another on the list of halting career moves I am sure. But he went to bed and Ron came over and said, "Holy fuck Ernie, I can't believe you did that.........that was fucking awesome."

When we got up in the morning we reported it, CQ Brian Anderson wasn't happy, but really it was just an accident.

As for me, I used all of my Infantry Stealth, Hiding and Disappearing training to hide my fucking ass from the WO until we headed into the field the next day. I wasn't in his Company and figured if I could only make it to the next day I would be safe for a few days and maybe it would just blow over.

Ya fucking right I was safe.

So now here we are in the middle of a Battalion Ex, moving forward in full attack with the carriers when over the radio comes,

"C Company Halt."

We stopped and opened the hatches to hear better. I was the track commander.

"The following people are to get into the back of this truck and head back to see the RSM (Regimental Sargent Major-The Boss)."

Oh fuck....

Well of course my name was the first to be called. "Okrainec put your 2 IC in charge," next name called was "Hayne,"....."I noted Hayne is my 2 IC,".....and was told "Well fucking put someone else in charge," "Allison," "McIntyre," "King"....etc.

Double fuck. Hoped it wouldn't be like the Great Escape, and taking us in the back of a truck into the Black Forest.

Now we rolled back to camp knowing we were likely up shit creek. Ya but the others in the crew also didn't do the picking up and chuck a WO thing either. Dumbfuck

So we waited in a field office for the RSM. I think it was The Baz in those days. Never had to meet him much but we all thought he was tough. Add to the fact he was also likely tired, not in a good mood and hadn't slept much. We just said we'd stick with the story of what happened. We each went in individually, and we could hear the conversation which was,

"Sir we are soldiers. If you were in our shoes and you were offered beer by a Senior NCO would you say no?"

Not sure if we did puppy eyes as well, but in the end it was the WO who paid the price and we were let off. He was a good guy who later finished his career with the PPCLI. In fact I just saw him a while back in Manitoba.

That's the thing about us. We are from all over so no matter what part of the country you are from if a message is sent out, a brother will let you know if they are in the area. It's pretty cool.

Get back to the Germany Story scatterbrain!!

Well it took him a few days, but the WO finally caught up with me. Couldn't hide forever. I apologized for fucking up and he didn't hold a grudge.

I also wasn't adding much as far as career advancement amendments to my file though.

When you finally got a break there was time for a cool one

Somewhere in the first couple of years I was a Sigs NCO. One day the Sigs Officer comes up to me and tells me that the RCR found codes in Transport Storage back in Winnipeg and that my name was assigned to them. This was a big no no, as the codes were secret documents used for communication. The only good thing was I didn't sign a Declaration that I destroyed them, as they were to be burnt after each exercise, or it would have been an even bigger shit storm. Oh and also we just got back from exercise and my Driver didn't secure his vehicle and Marg Security (The Marg was the area we worked on Base) opened the unlocked door and found the Secret Codes I was responsible for and for both incidents I was now being charged.

Now as I said before, when you fuck up, take your medicine. The codes in Winnipeg were mine. Just got buried somewhere and forgot about. The codes in the Carrier in Germany were not mine. Our 2 IC Captain insisted he sign for them to be important.

None the less I was charged, and received a Severe Reprimand and a $1,000 fine. Career halted for one year. I found out later it was a cover up and I was the fall guy. If I was then, the way I am now, I would have fought it once I found out it was the Captain who should have been charged. The Sigs Code NCO, where the codes were signed out from and also someone I considered at the time a buddy, was also told not to say a fucking word and to keep quiet by the Sigs O (Sigs Officer). You see they didn't want presented what really happened, but instead protect their own Officer and to hell with the truth. After all these years I am still bitter about it and also why, no matter where I have worked since, I don't let anyone walk over me. The Major who charged me knew who signed for these codes. That was his 2 IC. He was covering up for him and I was the carnage. I expected better from this Major considering his name had stature in the Regiment. But I wasn't going to win against the officers and for the most part I was fucked. Thus my trust issues with those of a higher rank or those in positions of power. This was abuse for sure.

As time after this incident started to be in the past it was then back to Canada, CFB Edmonton to be exact, for my Jump Course and the opportunity to get my wings. Like many of the other troops, I trained on my own in preparation for the course as it was quite physically demanding. In all there were about forty of us from the Battalion heading from Germany, so it was important to damn well make sure to be in good shape before starting the course as there was a PT Test when we arrived. If you failed you were done and immediately sent back to wherever you came from. The physical preparation was to focus mainly on upper body strength and we all pretty much worked out on our own. We all knew what was required as far as the physical demands.

So of course the night before we are flying to Canada I contacted a real bad flu and had a temp of 104F. On the way to Canada, not in the air but once landed, the plane broke down in Goose Bay, Newfoundland and we then had to fly via Herc the rest of the way to Edmonton. To say the least, we were on a plane for a very long time. We got in about 2:00 or 3:00 AM, were assigned rooms and had our PT test at around 7:00 AM. No rest for the wicked. The test included wind sprints to be done in a certain time, and chin-ups, push-ups and a few other things I can't remember. I did fine but was sure groggy for a couple of days until I started to feel better.

Prior to the start of the course, which had troops of all ranks from Officers to Privates, there was a separate meeting held for all of the higher ranks, in particular the Officers. They were told there was no rank as long as they were a candidate and essentially they would be treated like shit, just like the rest of us.

So what happens right off the bat, our Sgt. fails his chin-up test. Then for some reason our LT. refused to do his helmet push-ups and both were booted from the course. Well wasn't that a wasted trip across the world. And then, welcome to being in charge of the Platoon Ernie and Ed, as the other two were sent back and we were the Mcpl's, the next highest rank. Good thing it was a course where pretty much everyone looked after themselves, until they needed the emergency pay officer for something.

Anyone who has taken the course, and of course I know you Airborne guys would know best, it's a pretty physical course. No candidates are allowed to walk on the base, we had to run, we weren't allowed to walk in training buildings, we had to run, each time we entered the training building we had to do five chin-ups and each time we left the building, we had to again do five chin-ups. The instructors also made sure we were in and out of the training building quite a bit naturally. I'm not sure people, who haven't taken the course, realize just how many chin-ups we had to do each day. There were many many push-ups and upper body work as well in the racks (the training harnesses where we hung from the ceiling and practised parachute drills) with the harnesses up against our nuts, hanging there until they showed us later how to properly wear the harness. Jump Drills by the Jump Drills over and over.

The worst punishment though was the fucking Airborne Crawl. This was, while wearing our harness, being forced to drag your body (walking by your hands and dragging your feet) to wherever it was they told us we had to go. Now this wasn't dragging your carcass ten feet, it was quite a long of course and nothing was easy. The reward for finishing the Crawl was once we got to the end we then had to stand up, bend over with our legs straight, and touch our toes, with the muscles in our legs screaming. If you stood up you'd be toast and off the course. One time we came back in the building from outdoor training and saw the platoon from the Vandoo's (a platoon of them were going through the same time as us) sitting around looking miserable and we all noticed the tops of their boots scuffed, meaning they just finished the Crawl. We all knew what was coming for us. It was hard. It also wasn't fun being dropped from the racks, as we were swung in different directions, so we'd learn proper landings, which depended on which direction you were coming to the ground.

You know, normal office shit.

I also remember all the fireman carries. Now I'm not a small guy, but I was smaller compared to that baby ape Mac who I had to carry around. As a group we were matched up with partners and we were pretty much the two biggest guys, so thus he was my partner. He weighed about 260 plus. We were always near to last, but always got there. Funny that I just ran into him a while back at the Kapyong Base Tear down get together. Told him I still tell that story. Good laugh.

For the first two weeks of the course that was our routine. A few others dropped off but not many. It was repetition, repetition and more repetition so we would know our drills on the way out the door of the plane, and of course so we wouldn't freeze at the door. No one froze in our group that I recall.

One break that turned out pretty cool during the course was getting a tour of the facilities and running into a buddy I went through basic with who had become a rigger (they packed the parachutes). As a jumper you had trust in those guys.

Once we got past the first two weeks and passed to the jump phase, things became more normal and we were ready to jump. By normal I mean we weren't treated like crap anymore.

Out ya go

Well, all I can say is that jumping out of a plane is completely fucking awesome. Certainly not like the movies of steerable chutes and soft landings. We were jumping out with a 40 lb rucksack attached to our waist and steered by pulling the chute risers. It was damn awesome none the less. I remember seeing a picture of my first jump and looking for the green light with my eyes closed. But like everyone else, out the door I went.

What was even more cool was seeing all the open chutes in the sky, that was after I looked up to make sure my chute was open of course.

YEEEEHAAWW

It was a pretty damn free feeling looking down from 1,250 feet. I know it may not seem high, but that is until you are the one going out the door and steering for the right drop zone by your risers. We did have one guy land in rough plowed snow and dislocated his shoulder and many others with minor injuries, but that was part of the gig.

So now freedom and floating through the air aside, the ground is getting close and I let my rucksack loose and noticed the ground is coming quicker than I expected, "Oh fuck, thump, role, wiggle toes, all cool, bleeding nose, that was fuckin awesome can we go up again." Or words to that effect.

In all, we did six jumps, including one night jump, the fifth one. You passed if you got to that one. The first five jumps, I think, were side door jumps, and the last one was out the back of the ramp. The night jump may have been out the back of the plane, but it doesn't matter.

I remember the Jumpmaster saying prior to doing the night jump, "This is the night jump, well for some of you your fifth night jump as you fuckers haven't had your eyes open yet."

The night jump was pretty cool for sure. There were some reference points with lights on the ground, but fuck, it was night. I likely let the rucksack go early and knew once I heard it hit the ground I had about two seconds before I thundered in. In the end, if you walked away, it was a good jump.

The last jump was the best as you just walked to the back of the ramp and jumped, kind of like walking into a TV screen. There also wasn't the side wind action from the side door jumps that could twist the risers to the top so you would come down spinning the whole way, like happened to me in one of the jumps.

I remember one guy, who was from the Battalion but was posted at Jump School, bringing his chute in to be repacked along with the open reserve. The riggers got annoyed if you pulled the reserve by accident.

The Rigger asked, "'Why in the fuck did you pulled the reserve?"

His reply was, "Because I didn't want to fuckin die."

Guess his main didn't open.

So after three weeks, the bulk of us passed, proudly got our wings and it was back to Germany.

Like I said, when we had our time off, we found ways to have fun. What made it all better was the people we were with. They were there for the same thing and for the most part we sure stuck up for each other.

Well, in honor of all the snowballs (which was the code word for being bugged out), there was another that was a door to door snowball. The idea was you went house to house. The people whose door you knocked on had to provide drinks for everyone, then after the drink, you were to drop what you were doing, however you were dressed, and go with the group to the next house. You can imagine just how big the groups got after a few drunken hours. There was never the worry about serving the liquor because we all had lots, remember the ration cards. After ten or fifteen houses, the packs of people would be thirty to forty plus and pretty liquored, walking house to house singing. These snowballs were just a riot of fun.

We lived pretty close too many of the establishments and local watering holes. One night my ex was coming home and on the way back from Tiff's an army guy attacked her. I was home, it was close to our place and she ran in to tell me, and the hunt was on. I went to a couple of bars, including all night Benny's Balloon Bar, with about five buddies with me helping with the search. I didn't find him that night or even know who did it at this point, but about a week later a buddy came up and said he thinks he found out who it was. I didn't know the guy, but found out where he lived and waited that night in the shacks on base in another buddies room, as he wasn't in. He eventually came back and I confronted him and he admitted to it saying, "I didn`t mean it I was drunk."

I only hit him once, but he went down hard and was bleeding all over. It was a mess for sure. I told him I played broomball with his Major, which I did, and that I wanted a note of apology to my wife or I would be speaking with him. I then went home with blood on my shoes. It was also the first time I saw red and likely it was a good thing that he went down on the first shot as I'm not sure how far I would have went. I had been boiling mad for a week. It kind of worried me later as it could have turned out worse, but fortunately it didn't and I was satisfied the score was even.

I didn't hear much for a few days, but told the late Tim Downing about it as he was my Sgt. He said that explained why this guy was missing from whatever course he was instructing on. Guess he was taken to the hospital and had to stay for a few days. When he got out he gave me the note and that's all I did, and let it go. I did lose one buddy over it as this guy was in his section and he felt I could of handled it differently. My reply was, "We'll see how you'd fuckin handle things when it happens in your life." I never did get in trouble for it, but many people knew I did it. Not much they could really do because then they would be in a sense condoning the assault. But wasn't that how we were trained to handle things? Handle it like men. How many other fights and incidents like this happened? Sure it wasn't a career move again as this guy was a private, but fucked if I was just going to let it go. My buddies helped me resolve the issue and I would have done the same for them, and have, in a heartbeat.

Sports have always played a big part of my life, and it was no different over in Germany, and man we had opportunities if you played. I wasn't a hockey player for sure, and even though we were the Hockey Battalion, we had many other great sports teams. Probably the big three for me were fastball, broomball and football.

The Bandits

Johnny Juniper and I, along with few other guys, started the Bandits Fastball Team. There was a good league in Germany between the two bases, Lahr and Baden. The adventure obviously was the ride in the army whatever vehicle between the bases, especially on the way back. It was about an hour between the bases and cruising speed as to however fast the army vehicle could go. It was tough when we started the team, as we had a tight deadline, and we had one long practise and had to make cuts. In the end we had a really good squad of players. I can't remember for sure, but believe we were together for the last two years. The first year Johnny and I kind of coached, while the second year the Battalion assigned a couple of WO's to coach us as the word around was we were partying too much. This actually wasn't the case, but whatever. Well they didn't know much about fastball, but I was named captain and Johnny and I helped keep them in line, baseball wise, and things turned out fine. We made it to the final in our first year. Finished sixth in the Regular Season but made the playoffs upset everyone to the final. Can't remember who we lost too, but they were a good team. I still laugh as I have the team photo after we lost and when people from Germany see it they always ask if there were any pictures where people didn't have a killer Heineken in their hand. Fun times, lots of games and tournaments, and the boys were kind of your summer buddies. Some really great memories with a great bunch of guys and we played some really good ball.

I also played on the Base Team and got to travel with them. The best time was getting to go to London, England to play in a tournament on an American Base. What a time that was. The Baseball too!!! I can remember my parents and sister came to visit for a month and when they arrived and I had to leave in the next day or two to go to London for four days. My dad was a good fastball player in his day and thought it was pretty cool.

So the first night in London was a free night and the five or six of us infantry guys who made the team were drinking somewhere that didn't matter. Tommy got into the Mad Dog and after way to much of that I understood why it was called Mad Dog, as he turned rabid. Well when he woke up any way. We first dragged him back to barracks and wore the tops of his shoes off. He woke up in the bathroom, punched a mirror, cut himself, and started swinging at Punch and I. Each swing missed but the blood didn't. So our white ball uniforms were full of blood. He finally calmed down and Punch grabbed our uniforms and it was quick to the laundry before the blood dried. Tommy didn't look too good the next day and sat on the bench with his scratched sunglasses on all day. Fun times. The ball competition was awesome as well and great to take part in. I remember we made the playoffs. I also remember leaving my seven day old $500 suit pants behind because we slept in the next morning prior to heading back for our flight. Must have been because we were out all night for some reason. I also remember we were trying to keep the American bus driver awake when he was driving us to the airport as he was partying with us and was falling asleep driving the bus. Somehow we made it back in one piece just in time for the Hugey Beer Tent, so we got by.

From the beginning of the tour I was also on the broomball team. We started the team the year prior to going to Germany and not many of us on the team knew much about broomball. I recall we were on exercise in Shilo, Manitoba before the Germany Tour and the Battalion arranged a game against the artillery team in front of our Battalion. We were out on exercise and didn't have much of our sports gear and even had a bunch of guys playing the game in mukluks not broomball shoes. Our goalie was in the bag, we weren't very good and we got shit kicked 10-0. Once we got to Germany we kept at it, got in really good shape so no one could run us down, and eventually got to be a contender every year. The next year we went to Edmonton to play in Strong Contender (which was the Western Military Sports Competition). The tournament also included the Battalion Hockey and Volleyball Teams. Of course the Hockey Team won, they were pretty damn good. We watched their games but were closer to the Volleyball Crew and really supported each other. I mean really bonded well partying with each other.

We won our first game in Edmonton but our Coach, CSM Collier, wasn't happy we partied the night before and CB'd (Confined to Barracks) us. The next day we played like shit losing one and tied the other but we squeezed into the playoffs. So, that night he took us out and got us pissed so we would play better the next day and we won the quarter-final, the semi-final and lost in the final against the same guys who beat us 10-0. We lost 1-0. We really out played them but they kept us off the sheet and they scored on a rebound. It was great broomball and great bunch of guys. Man we had fun, especially those van trips back and forth from Baden to Lahr. Whoever wasn't driving just poured out of the van upon our return, cans rolling around, "Too victory!!!!"

Also broke some bones in that sport. Broke my collar bone, that still hasn't healed, and my hand, that certainly I feel when the weather is changing. We had another CSM who coached us throughout the tour who also really stuck up for us, and also the late Tim Downing who was a good coach as well. I got to Captain the team, and we had a great group of guys who had pride and worked hard to win for the Battalion.

As soldiers we also very much loved Military Medicine (lol). I broke my collar bone getting cross checked in a broomball game. Being we were in Baden, they didn't take care of this type of thing at the hospital on base for some reason so I had to go to the hospital in Lahr. As I couldn't even take my jersey off, I got Doug Harding had to drive me, drinking to numb the pain of course. So I get there and get an x-ray and the doc says,

"It looks like your broke your collar bone in the past, there is a break here."

I said, "Ummmm no, that's why I'm here, I just broke it."

His reply was, "No, this looks old and doesn't look like it just happened."

"Christ man, I just broke it playing broomball, I have never broke it before."

"Are you sure this just happened?"

Geez man, military medicine at its finest.

So in the end they put me in a figure eight wrap, it hurt like hell, so took it off when I got back to the parking lot, and of course it never healed properly. I still can't sleep on that side, but hey it was worth it for the story. The Military didn't take injuries well so I didn't want to be labeled as a wimp and just carried on. No wonder my bones are better at predicting weather changes now.

A few of us Infantry guys also played on the Base Team (the Base Team was the team made up from anyone on the base and harder to get on). There was also a yearly play down against the Lahr Base to see who would go back to Canada for Nationals. Now while it was good to make the team, it was particularly annoying that the coaches had obvious preference to the Air Force guys, whom they knew better than us Infantry guys. It's also why there were three Artillery guys who played on our Pat's Team, because they we getting screwed by the Base side gang who ran the team. Anyway, one year we made it to Nationals in Ottawa. Went all the way from Germany, and that fucker didn't play the Infantry guys for the first three games. We were pissed off for sure and didn't show up for the last game. We even went out and bought our own three amigo jerseys and wore them around. It was good broomball though for sure. If you are from the Quebec area you'll know what I mean because the teams from there were pretty damn good at broomball.

Run Forrest Run

Football was an annual fall tradition within the Battalion, as much as Broom-i-loo (a game of broomball on grass between teams from each Company played each Regimental Birthday from which bones are usually broken somewhere during the games.) It pitted each Company Team against each other and there were some pretty awesome rivalries. There was one company that once brought back the starting QB from whatever training he was on just for the tournament. It was important for Company bragging rights.

This was flag football where as long as you came up with the flag, even if it meant breaking someone's body part, football. I was on the winning team one of the years in Germany. Usually was the QB, but also played Middle LB and Kicker. I was a decent player for our league, but so were many others. The year we won we were so good no one scored on us the entire season and we had a good offense. In the final the team we played against tried to punt for a single on the last play just to say they scored, but we blocked it. That same team beat us in the final the next year in a close game they deserved to win. Tough football and you went for beers after and told stories, then would laugh your ass off.

Champs

Champs

The last couple of years I organized the entire mini season and playoffs, and doing a good job I was getting back into better graces. Geez that's what happens when you keep your mouth shut, fathom fucking that. Don't worry it didn't always stay that way.

I was a good athlete among a Battalion that had many good athletes. Let's face it, we were infantry, so pretty much all of us could run, including in pain or hungover. We had some really great athletes depending on the sport.

It can't go without saying though that our Battalion was the hockey Battalion and the team was built to win while we were in Germany. In fact they won the Championship all four years. Hockey was big around there and games were broadcast on the radio. Man it was some good hockey to watch and I got over the fact that the players got more benefits than us. Heck we had a guy who topped my Section Commanders Course back in Winnipeg, which was a short course as it was, who was a hockey player and got to miss much of the training to go to hockey. When we were doing our patrols on the course he was my navigator (using the compass to lead us where we needed to go), and I had to take over as he wasn't going the right way. In the end if I could have played hockey I would have played as well. Had many buddies on that team and they were good guys. A couple guys went on to play in the German League.

There was once kind of a trade being made with one of our PPCLI Battalions where we sent our best shooter to them for their Biathlon Team for a hockey player to come and join the team in Germany. It was a guy many of us know as his brother played in the NHL. So he noted, "Ya I can play hockey," and they sent him to Germany and then he said, "Well I didn't say I was very good.", or so the story goes. Ah Brian, had some great laughs with him.

The team did the Battalion proud no matter what you thought. To win every year, the games were an event.

We also had an annual track and field meet between both bases Lahr and Baden. I was usually on the forced march team or something of that nature as I wasn't the top guy in any particular event, just decent at many. Like I said we had some good athletes. As a Battalion we always finished second. I can't remember who always won, maybe Service Battalion, but they had more depth. Track meets had come a long way from the Winnipeg days when there used to be a beer tent at the meet. If an event was later in the day, guys could be pretty hammered, with some even running their race backwards. Then again in Germany we usually went to some Beer Tent after.

I also ran a marathon over there with Bill Brown. We were in good shape from Sigs and I thought the marathon gave me a medal when I finished. What could go wrong? So we did pretty well and ran the 42 kms and rolled to the finish line where I was now expecting my medal but instead I got a fuckin certificate. The 10 km race got the medal. And to boot my butt cheeks were on fire from hair rash and I walked to the beer garden like I had a pickle up my ass. But it turned out I kept this certificate longer than any medal because we had a ton of medals from various activities.

RICHARD (ERNIE) OKRAINEC

I'm a Marathon Man

But I'll tell you my ass was this hot;

With major butt burn

It was the road trips that were a hoot playing sports. Laughing your asses off, cruising as fast as you can on the autobahn. For me if there was a sport I'd give it a try. I was decent at badminton and volleyball as well.

We also had a really good Soccer Team who won Canadian Nationals, a really good Rugby Team, who were also really good a partying hard as well, which is what you did in Rugby.

Sports occasionally got us out of exercises if we had a major tournament or something of that nature. Not always, but sometimes. It was interesting going to the RI Club (The Room International-Main Base Bar) when all the boys were in the field. Sure were lots of Air Force guys at the bar who weren't there before when the boys were in town.

Through all the dirt and mud we also cleaned up well for either parades, drill competitions and of course Remembrance Day.

We cleaned up well for parades

The thing about being in Germany was the opportunity to have lots of visitors. I felt since I was in Europe I'd only go back for courses, so really had a ton of family and friends come by. All the boys treated everyone great, like we did when their family or friends came to visit.

My parents and sister came for a month and we had a great time. The first day they arrived, like anyone who did that long flight, they were messed up from jet lag. I picked them up at the airport in Frankfurt a few days after it was bombed from a terror attack, which wasn't as common back then, and gave them their first shit scared experience of the autobahn. The one where I did the one finger driving at 160, something they weren't used to for sure. So like all of us who were used to travelling on long distance flights, if you landed, say in the morning, from the overseas flight you would try and stay awake to try and get on regular time. It's always a plan anyway.

The first day when they arrived I was playing a triple header of fastball in prep for our London Tourney trip. My dad played fastball all his life so he came right away. The first game he was pretty quiet. Later, while I was playing, I see my army buddies, who knew him from our Winnipeg days, show up. Next I see Ted carrying a bag of beer and Terry a bag of ice. By the end of the second game he was cheering pretty loud. By the middle of the third game I didn't hear anything and found out they had to take him home. Mom said they dropped him off and he was bouncing off the walls. Welcome to Germany. He missed supper.

But that's how it was. The boys always wanted to meet your family. Let's face it we were from everywhere. They partied and looked after our family, like us theirs.

I did warn my dad that he had to be careful, as there was a kidnap group. All in fun of course, but kidnappers none the less. They would convince your dad to come out for a drink and then bugger off somewhere with him for a couple days. You'd just get a cryptic call that they had him and he was safe. Funny stuff, unless you were booked to head out on vacation and they wouldn't bring him back. Well one day he got the call for him to go for a drink of course, but he declined.

We all took visitors to lots of places. The awesome thing was, even with many different visitors we didn't have to go to the same places, as there was so much to see throughout Europe. Of course the nude beaches caught their attention for sure, especially taking the family to Italy. Pretty much all beaches in Europe were topless beaches. Dad would lay on the beach cot playing it cool, until the ladies and my mom went swimming, and he was quickly up with his zoom lens taking topless pictures. He found a big chubby girl in his camera sights and said, "This one's for your uncle Teddy," then he quickly laid back down before the ladies returned, like nothing happened.

Ahhh...the topless and nude beaches of Europe. We had a nude quarry that was close to base. Used to joke that someone could always tell when the Canadians first arrived to Germany and were doing their first trip to the nude quarry. They'd have sunburnt asses and there would be a hole in the sand. Was certainly different being at the quarry and seeing your neighbour doing what you were doing. Such was life in Europe and we all got used to it.

We took them too many places and countries, as that was what we did, we travelled. Mom and Dad had a running joke to get lucky in every country. Someone even forgot their panties in Switzerland. We were driving back from Italy, through Austria, but not staying overnight, just driving through, and someone was trying to get lucky at a parking lot. Well everyone should have goals in life!!!! My buddy Ted came with us. After driving about six or eight hours I got Ted to drive so I could have some rest. Ten minutes later, while trying to get a nap on the floor of the van, I hear an argument as he's now stuck in a big roundabout and couldn't figure out how to exit and, just like European Vacation, we kept going round and round. I ended up driving again. We laughed our asses off.

Had another family crew come for a month during Oktoberfest and Fasching (basically a one month Halloween Party with many awesome events throughout the month). It was good timing for a visit and we partied for much of the month with all the events going on, including Oktoberfest in Stuttgart. Geez could write a chapter just on Oktoberfest. What a blast.

One night a couple of the boys put together a big Halloween costume party. We decided to go as a six pack of Heineken. We worked on those costumes for a long time, drinking and laughing all the way. We ended up winning first prize. Even carried Fred on to the stage in a coffin as Blue Hiway was playing. There certainly were some funny costumes. One guy came dressed as a piece of shit. Painted brown with peanuts glued on him.

Friends, family, boy we a ton of visitors, once they were all added up. Sometimes though, in Military fashion, we didn't get to enjoy the visit as we'd be called out with no notice. This happened a few times for sure. Get a visitor but then off to the field and didn't get to see them.

During the visits the company always had trouble sleeping at first with the F-18's and 104's buzzing around. The rest of us were already used to them by then.

F-18's buzzed around on a regular basis

The 104's were nicknamed the lawn dart for a reason. They kind of looked like one. During the tour one went down with a pilot, who was tragically killed. The farmer said he heard something like mud squishing and went out and the side of his barn was covered in mud. During the recovery they dug down about twenty to thirty feet before they started finding signs of the plane and pilot. Was certainly a sad day on the base for sure.

And to lighten things up again;

Man, I can't get into more without telling the Body Building Competition story with Johnny Pirola being entered.

So I believe it was our third year of the tour and the Base was putting on a body building competition. There was one of the boys from the Battalion who was seriously entered along with quite a few from around the base. So turns out drinks in the bar and a bet led to the boys entering Johnny. Now Johnny was not small but was thin and very hairy. They practised, all oiled up at our bar, the CC (the Canadian Club which pretty much was just our unit), where he'd stand on a table and Rob McDonald, I believe, would call out numbers of various poses and he would do them. We laughed our asses off. So the day of the competition finally arrives and we pile into the theatre. The curtain opens to the first few muscled contestants, then it opens to the mighty Johnny, all oiled up and hairy and ready to go. All of the other contestants were bulked up and Johnny, well, was the thin hairy guy. We gave him a standing ovation. The judges laughed and told him he could stop flexing. Eventually the curtain wrapped around him and he was dragged pretty much off the stage. The organizers weren't happy. We left, went back to the bar and laughed out asses off.

RICHARD (ERNIE) OKRAINEC

The Legend of Johnny

There was a time to be serious, but when we didn't have to be, we weren't.

Early in the second year the bulk of the Battalion was called into the Base Theatre. We were to be addressed by some senior officer, who was an Air Force guy, whose title I do not recall, but he kept track of formal charges throughout the forces. Turns out he wasn't happy and was giving us a lecture, well not a lecture, he was pissed off. He told us we had just set the base record for the most impaired driving charges, and not only that, but the record for the most in the entire armed forces. He didn't get the reaction he was expecting. There was a brief silence then we gave out a big cheer followed by chants of, "We`re number 1, We're number 1." He wasn't impressed and stormed off the stage left.

We did have quite a few of the boys, at first, who got impaired charges. I was one the ones who did not, but it could have happened too many of us. The Base really did try and curb these types of things by providing what we called, "The Drunk Bus". This was having someone on duty who, after being called, would come via van and pick us up so we wouldn't drink and drive. Many of us did use that service, though sometimes we'd have to wait quite a while for the van to show up as it was picking up troops from all over the place in the various towns.

Because It Was The Truth

Life in garrison wasn't always fun at work as between training we did a lot of mundane tasks, like pound track or clean gear or area sweeps etc. So if we ever got a chance to be temporarily away from the Battalion many of us would jump at the chance.

While on our base the chance for us was Base Defense Force. This was where a small group of people spent a month over on the Base Side away from the unit, which really was the other side of the base, and where everyone else who wasn't Infantry worked. BDF was the group who provided base defense and this group was attached with the Base MP's. The basics were to patrol the Base in Vans on shiftwork twenty four hours a day and work twelve hour shifts. It also included many days off during the month, which was great, as we were not with the Battalion for those thirty days and we could do whatever we wanted on those off days. The job was both slack and could be crazy as well if something actually happened. Nothing happened during my stint.

Well as you can imagine being Infantry and working over with the Base Meathead's wasn't fun as they didn't like us and we didn't like them. They somehow thought they owned us and could treat us however they wanted. Some Corporals got a bit lippy and I had to remind them who the Mcpl was. There was also a few of my buddies there as well doing some time in base jail. I would make a point to go over to talk to them in the cell and the MP would come and try and chew me out like I was some dog.

I would just say, "Listen Corporal, if you keep talking to me in an insubordinate way you'll be joining him in the next cell. Clear?" He then buggered off pissed off.

During that stretch we worked long hours for sure, but also ended up with seventeen days off. It was awesome punishment to be away from Battalion.

It was funny though, as the people who were given that duty from the Air Force side looked at it as being punished, while the army guys celebrated being away from the Battalion for a month. You could tell we lived different lives.

Of course we made the night shift fun. We patrolled the Base, the Marg and Runways in vans. So when it was slow through the night we'd play hide and seek driving around with the lights off throughout the woods, along the runway and all over the back forty. Sure made the nights go quicker and had a lot of fun dodging the MP's who'd be chasing us around but couldn't catch us. You can imagine what we did for our days off. It was a great month and really was a drag when we had to go back to Battalion.

He wasn't a wog, turned out to be an artillery brother, Rick Huskilson

Somewhere along the line I went from a Rifle Company to Signals Platoon. I was also sent back to Gagetown for my Advance Communications Course (learning pretty much anything and everything of all the communication equipment, procedures, antennas and codes). The course was lots of classroom. I remember getting to our room where we would be living during the course and three of us PPCLI guys, Glen Evans, Jess Adair and myself, shared a room. We also put up a sign on our door which said, "No Wogs Allowed." Wogs were basically anyone who wasn't infantry. It was funny as most people who were on the course and living in the same building didn't come in as they didn't know what to think of us, except for one Artillery guy, Rick Huskilson. He also made the flight from Germany to the course. Well, we became fast friends. Later back in Germany he, along with a couple others from his Artillery Squad came to play on our broomball team, and we are still very close friends to this day. We even went fishing every May long weekend for twenty five years after he retired. Rick was also our entertainment on the course as he tried very hard to get kicked off as he didn't want anything to do with Advance Comms. I used to laugh as he would fail a test on purpose and they would pass him anyway. I thought, geez man, I guess I am going to pass this fucking course. The problem was it was taught by Tankers and the radio set up in a tank was different than ours, and of course we didn't like each other. What a shock. In any event I passed after eight weeks or so. Man, I also had some great laughs with Brian Semenko. He also didn't take kindly to the tankers and told them off lots. Not Brian right? So the day we got our certificates for passing the course, he gets his, marches to the door, does and about face, rips it up and chucks it in the garbage. We laughed our asses off.

We, of course, also got into our fair share of trouble. On our way back from the course we almost missed our plane as we partied all night and had to sprint to the gate sweating our asses off to catch the plane. We forgot all our books in the room. We then got to Ottawa and were bumped off Service Air and found out we would be flying back to Germany via Lufthansa the next day. Fathom our luck, from flying Service Air in full uniform to a civilian airline. Our uniforms were quickly discarded and stuffed in the suitcase and we called the Emergency Pay Officer as we were stranded. He asked how much we needed and we took about $500 each. His jaw kind of dropped. That last thing I remember that night was Brian's head banging against the vending machine as he was trying to put in the wrong amount of money for the 3:00 AM Cheetos.

Let's face it, compared to Service Air, Lufthansa was awesome. Certainly way more comfortable, and the drinks were free, for the entire ten hour flight. Well we kept the stewardesses busy the whole way back, kind of like the Avon ding. They'd even bring two at a time but we'd still call.

So likely not many people back in Germany knew we got bumped from the flight and just when we'd be getting to the Frankfurt airport. So we did what we knew best and went to the bar in the airport to figure out how we were going to get back to base. About an hour later a driver showed up and said he figured he'd find us there and was told to pick us up. We used the last of our emergency pay to pay for our round. Where'd my field pay go!!!

As I mentioned, the Military can be cruel to its soldiers as well. I had a brother I went through with who I won't mention by name. When I got to know him through Basic and Infantry training and as my first roommate when I got to Battalion, I knew he had issues at home. He was sending the majority of his money back home to support his single mother and sister. As a private certainly it wasn't like we had much money, but he sent everything he could.

We eventually drifted apart but I knew he was stressed. I was back home one day when we were still in Winnipeg and found out he tried to commit suicide. He was found in his room with his slashed wrists in a bucket of water. It had all got to him, the pressure. Fortunately someone found him in time and saved his life. He went away for quite a while and one day showed back up in Battalion while we were on exercise. I was a Mcpl by then. He was treated like a leper by the higher ranks for sure, and that, in my mind, wasn't fucking fair. As I was a Signs NCO, I was somewhat close with a CSM who we were working with and I asked him if I could take him under my wing while trying to explain some of the issues he was going through. He said, "OK", and with that I helped get him through for a while. He even made it to the posting in Germany.

Sometime during the tour he went AWOL (Absent Without Leave) and was missing for over a week. I hadn't seen him much during this time as we were in different companies, but I was concerned as he took a dark path with drugs and he was pretty addicted. Many of us weren't angels and bullshitting if many said they were, but he was way down the wrong road with them, which happens. I always found it odd if you ended up being an addict you were a treated like the bottom scum of the earth, but if you were an alcoholic, well that was ok and you were treated different. So then one day while he was AWOL he turned up at my place. Well now I was in a pickle, as he really had to turn himself in, but he didn't want too and wanted to stay with me. He was in rough shape. We talked for quite a while and he finally agreed to let me take him in to the Base to turn himself in to the MP's. He was sent to rehab somewhere after that. I didn't get a chance to go see him again, as basically the next day we went to the field for six weeks. I was told he was calling for me and even made me a model car with his shaking hands. I felt really bad but there was nothing I could do. He was sent back to Canada and spit out of the system and the Military and I never saw him again. All I can say is that I hope he survived his demons and that he's still around. I Miss him.

I went to Sigs Platoon during the last half of the tour at a really good time. It wasn't the typical Sigs from back in Winnipeg, which isn't meant as an insult. Sigs Platoon was a mix of Infantry guys and Sigs trade troops. As a mixed group of trades we were very close, which through my stories you may have noticed, we didn't always play well with others. This was not the case with this group.

We were like another rifle platoon as far as being in shape and being trained like others in rifle companies. Just our jobs were different, as we supplied the battalion and when we were in the field we weren't at the front. The reason we were in great shape was the fact we were led by the late Jim Decoste as the Platoon WO, then after that it was Rui Amaral. There was no one not in shape in that Platoon, including the Sigs trades who were with us. It was a really great crew and a great bunch of guys.

We knew we were pretty good from the Battalion Forced March Competition which everyone took part in throughout the Battalion. This was a yearly competition which was a ten mile race with all our gear, including Machine Guns, Anti-tank weapons and the like. After the run there was a skills competition.

Some of the boys in training. We ran in the Black Forrest

Now putting Marching in the name of the competition was like when I thought having Light in the PPCLI name would work out fine. We weren't Marching, we were hauling ass. The race was a damn tough course to run on. Somewhere along the route I remember about two miles of tank track which was all little hills and sand that we had to run on. Man after that and finally hitting the hard pavement of the road it was like a holiday.

In those days it was always a close race between us and Recce Platoon, but they usually won the overall. I think we were pretty even in the race portion and fell to second or third after the skills part. We sure were good runners though. The skills competition consisted of things such as shooting, grenade throwing, range cards and those types of things. For the race part there was competition between us and Recce where some Officers were betting who would win, as we were both pretty damn fast. For us it was a friendly competition with Recce, and the Rifle Platoons as well. A lot of those guys in Recce were my buddies too. Good on them, but I was pretty proud of our Sigs group, a mix of Infantry and Sigs Trades. Who would have thought we'd be as good as we were. Of course our nickname was "Sigs Pigs".

Mean Sigs bastards from the forced march competition

We were all in shape because we ran or walked everywhere in those days. PT in the morning was no cake walk. Worse if hung over. Both Jimmy and Rui had the same rule. Didn't care what we did at night, but we'd better be there in the morning. Same when we were on the training bases. There were no vehicles to take us to the ranges, so we had to hump it a few miles or more. We walked everywhere to get where we needed to go. Everyone walked or ran to the ranges from the Battalion.

As a side note, people ask why we sang so much. It passed time on the long runs or humps we all had to do.

I still have a picture coming back from the ranges when Jimmy had us walk back in State 3, with full suit and gas masks. It was hot that day, but really fucking hot walking in a rubber suit with a gas mask on, as anyone who has done this will attest. We still had water breaks and fresh air breaks where we took off the masks, but we were soaking fucking wet with sweat when we got back. None of us complained though, we were all doing it, including Jimmy.

State 3 was always fun

After the training for those forced march competitions I was likely in the best shape of my life for sure. I'm sure it was the same for many others in our platoon. Worked hard and partied hard when we got the chance.

Back at home base I remember Rui getting the idea we would ride our mountain bikes to the city of Baden Baden from the base, which certainly was a ways away, and go to the baths. Baden was known for its baths and Casino's. So there were quite a few of us who volunteered, (was another one of those you win if you volunteer things), and over a dozen of us hit the road and headed out on our Mountain Bikes. So we eventually ended up at the nude baths. We got undressed and went up to the second floor bar to hang out after we did the baths. After a while we ordered drinks and went to pay and it was then you realized there is no wallet in your back pocket as we were buck ass naked. Well someone paid but I really don't want to know where the money was stuffed or tucked or where it came from. We laughed our asses off. Was a crazy fun day and then rode the bikes back.

Biking back to return to Base we used the same side roads we took on the way to our adventure of the day. Well in vehicles, everyone drove fast everywhere, even in places they weren't supposed to be going fast. Well this guy, who happened to be the CO, was driving his car to fast and almost hit us coming around a curve. It was ironic on parade later he made some rule where we weren't to be out on the roads on bikes. Ya, like we were the ones speeding where you weren't supposed to be speeding. That's how it always seemed to work.

When we travelled whether it was on exercise or on vacation we were treated pretty well as Canadians in Europe. This was even more so in Holland and Belgium who have never forgotten what Canadians did for them during the war. It's too bad, for the most part, Canada doesn't remember. Now it seems people are too worried about offending someone. Many of the things we had the opportunity to see were some things we had only heard or read about. When in Amsterdam I went to Anne Frank's house, well the tiny attic they had hid in for a very long time until they were ratted out and sent to a Concentration Camp. Also visited the Van Gough Museum, drinking Heineken on tap as that's where the factory is…oh and there was this place called The Bulldog.

It was hard to believe how accommodating the majority of the German's were to us when we were on exercise, considering we actually may be set up in their yard, usually with large vehicles or tracks. Many a time we would be set up with whatever we were doing and someone would bring out some goodies from their house. There was one particularly funny time when I was back with Charlie Company and Tiny was in the middle of giving us a lecture of how we were going to soldier, that we'd be eating rations only and there would be no drinking, then in mid-sentence the owner came out with two cases of beer and a rack of sandwiches for us. Tiny just said, "Fuck," and walked away. We laughed our asses off and enjoyed. Couldn't be rude eh!

When I was moved within our platoon from Sigs Transport over to Sigs Stores my digging trenches life was pretty much over as I was in A Ech and supplied the Battalion with gear as needed. The rifle companies usually came to us at the rear where we got them resupplied and fixed or replaced broken equipment. Usually I slept in the back of my covered MLVW, off the ground, dry and with a stove to heat up the place. For the most part we got to eat in restaurants or from the bread trucks. We still had sentry and such, but not to the extent of the rifle platoons and company's for sure. When we had to go out and supply the Battalion we did. We'd find where they were and did our thing, but certainly it was a far cry from the rifle company days living in the cold and digging trenches. Wiggling my toes was no longer required. In Sigs the guys who had to lay the line to keep communications up worked their asses off nonstop. They'd just get, say, forty miles of line down to get everyone in contact, then the Battalion would move to a new location and they would have to pick it back up and start again. We'd run into them once in a while and they would be bagged from the long hours. This included my good buddy Clay Rankin, Henry Bedard, Steve Christo, Dwayne Clayton and a few others. Those guys worked their asses off for long stretches of time. I mean were talking some thirty to forty miles or more of line. They'd lay it down, pick it up, repeat each time we'd move to another location.

And my good buddy Clay Rankin

Back when I was a younger Sigs NCO still in Winnipeg and I had to lay the line for the Company, and the job was to do it on my own, like every other Company Signs NCO. I humped the big spool with about a mile of line on it through the snow or whatever terrain and weather to get everyone connected. One day I was hooking up the phone with the line wrapped around my hands, when somewhere someone drove over the line I had laid with a military snowmobile. The driver wasn't paying attention and line got caught up in the track. So when that happened, with the line wrapped around my hands, all of a sudden I was being dragged out of the tent, just like a cartoon, until I got my hands out of my gloves. Too funny. Another time, during the same exercise, I learned the hard way not to put the spliced line in my mouth. I had spliced the line to hook up in the phone and was doing something and put the bare ends in my mouth, then at that time someone rang up their field phone from the other end and lit me up. We laughed our asses off, though I laughed more when the numbness went out of my lips.

Get back to Germany you idiot or you'll never finish this friggen book.

Lady Patricia always came to see the troops

Back to Germany, I really took to the job of Sigs Stores and liked it, and I was good at it. It was a good way to spend roughly the last year and a half in Germany. We sure had some really good people in Sigs who made it gung ho and fun. It was also during the majority of that time I got my shit together. We had a couple of Sig Officers when I was there, who weren't Infantry but in charge of the Platoon. The second one told me if I worked for him he'd look after me, as others heard over their time in the military as well. So I did. I worked hard and did well in this job. As a group though, we were more led by Jimmy and Rui being they were infantry guys. But that's what I did, kept my nose clean, and all my write-ups were 8's, 9's and 10's out of 10 all year. When it was performance review time Rui told me I was ranked number one for Mcpl's after his Senor NCO's rankings, which meant a chance of promotion. Shortly after when I met with the Sigs Officer for my yearly evaluation I was rewarded with a seven for my work, which meant going nowhere. He gave me all the bullshit excuses and certainly I was pissed off. I realized the truth of it was, I wasn't going anywhere in my career no matter how hard I worked and it pissed me off. I wasn't the only one this happened to though. It was then I decided I would be getting out once we were done in Germany, though I didn't mention it to anyone and had my first thoughts about pursuing a career in the media. But at the time it was just a thought as I still had a tour to finish.

As with all of us, we had a visit from the Career Manager as the tour was coming to an end. This was an Officer assigned to go over options with the troops for things like changing trades, postings and going over your career in general. After this tour a great many of the troops would be changing trades, getting out or getting posted elsewhere when we got back to Canada as a Battalion of that size wouldn't be required.

During my one on one interview he certainly was very respectful, and noted my sports pedigree. He went over the various aspects of my career but especially reviewed all the teams I played on, my organizing of tournaments for the Battalion and also pulled the note from my file from way back when I was recruited about my interest in being a Peri. I was informed that I was very highly recommended to finally get the trade I entered the forces wanting to do, a Peri. I was also given a course date should I want to proceed. It was everything I originally wanted.

Well, I was still not over what happened during my last evaluation, quite pissed actually, and I said. "Thanks, but I decline the opportunity," and that was the end of that. I was the only one at that point who knew my plan.

So as this tour of Germany was coming to a close, likely the four most influential years of my young life, good and bad, we were now preparing to go back to Canada.

After all the amazing training, the travel, the lifetime of memories, meeting Nazi's, getting up to the Eagles Nest, seeing the remains of Death Camps, touring underground bunkers, getting to tour the Maginot Line (Hitler's last line of defense), living on many trains and road moves, eating and drinking at all the establishments of wherever we were, enjoying the beauty of Europe from England to Italy, the posting was at an end and it was time to go home.

I found out I would be heading back advance party to help get the base ready back in Winnipeg with a contingent of other troops. We went back about three months prior to the rest of the Battalion.

Now in the military they never teach anyone how to actually save money and we truly did spend most of it. We all were under the assumption we'd be taken care of when we retired. But when we got posted, we got paid.

When posted there were movers hired by the military to pack and move everything we owned. These things, including vehicles if they were being kept, were packed and put in crates to be shipped back and were not seen again for quite a few weeks. As a result we were all put up in hotels for extended periods of time, both prior to posting and when back in Winnipeg, until housing arrangements were made. For me I was in a hotel three weeks before we left Germany and about a month more in Canada. If I remember right, we got $400 Canadian a week for the hotel and another $400 a week for food, plus a month's pay posting allowance. This was on top of regular pay. I also had a loan at the Sparkasse Bank for the Audi. I wasn't bringing it back as it didn't meet Canadian emission standards, and would have cost a lot to be converted. The other thing was back in Canada you'd rarely drive out of third gear. I bought a VW rabbit the last few months just to try and slow down. So with the loan, it turned out the bank took off additional money each month as security for the loan and invested it, but when the loan was paid off I got the investment back with interest. I thought it would be a few hundred marks, but it was in fact about $8,000. Holy shit, I was loaded, and better than field pay. Of course we all used much of it to buy things to bring home and spent a lot having fun.

Tell me then that the CanEx (the Base Wal-Mart I suppose as it had everything) on any base wasn't a place to print money. We spent so much money there getting things duty free from furniture to stereos to cameras to pretty much anything you can think of.

The hardest thing to get rid of really was the booze, as for the most part we weren't bringing it back. But everyone pretty much had ten full bottles kicking around of hard liquor and whatever else from beer to wine to shooters. The people in the towns we lived in benefitted the most, and really they should have. They were very good to us. So the bankers, the landlords, the people in the Gasthaus, the friends we met, got all the liquor.

As for the movers, well we had to watch out for them for sure as to just what they would pack. They were on a mission to pack, and packed everything when no one was looking. I had one buddy who had the dirty baby diaper pail packed. I can't imagine what their crate smelt like after six to eight weeks. Uggh. Probably was worse than how I smelled back in Fort Reilly.

So at the end prior to leaving we were put up in a hotel down the street. The night before leaving I went back to the apartment to do one final check after we had cleaned the place, just to make sure I didn't leave anything. So I opened the door and there was an RCR guy, the Battalion taking over from us, trashing my place. Throwing stuff on the floor and making a mess. I asked what the fuck he was doing there and kicked him out. I cleaned up whatever mess he made, was pissed off, and after I was finished putting the place back together I didn't think much about it. Well that was until I was at the airport the next day and got pulled aside by some officer asking why I left my place a shit pit. Of course it wasn't true but it turned out the RCR guy went back and finished his work after I left. He was with their advance party and they wanted someone to make an example of as to how not to leave your place. This was bullshit of course. Well as I was ready to get on the plane I couldn't defend myself. The Officer seemed like he was going to charge me but Brian Anderson, the CSM, vouched for me that he knew me and knew I wouldn't leave my place like that. Which was true of course and the Officer walked away.

Well turns out that didn't matter and I found out when I was back in Canada that the CO was using me as an example on parade with the Battalion as to how not to leave your housing. Of course I was across the ocean and couldn't defend myself again. Now I was even more livid. When I found out this was happening, that was fucking it, and I put in for my release (to leave the Military) that day. Putting in your release took about six months, and really the timing was perfect as the Battalion wasn't around for another three months, and by the time they were back to doing full Battalion duties I would be pretty much finished, with only about a month to go. Which is how it all turned out in the end.

Coming back to Winnipeg was a struggle financially for sure. Not initially, as we had the posting funds and those things, but once settled a month or two in, we realized there was a lot less money on the paycheque. When posted overseas we received in and around an extra $1,000 a month for living expenses. Well now all of that was gone and no longer part of the pay cycle, and generally it was much more expensive to live in Canada compared to Germany. We were now without our perks of duty free and rations cards and such. It was the reality of not saving a heck of a lot in those days. The horror. It took a while to adjust and we all tried to warn the boys when they got back about what life would be like as far as money.

But life in Battalion back in Canada with just the advance party was pretty grand. Being in Sigs our office and buildings were actually off the main base and just down the road. While there was an Officer and a WO with us it was basically Clay Rankin and I who did the turnover with the RCR and got ready for the boys to come back. The first thing we did was move our Officers Office down to Headquarters, which was on the base far from us, and noted how important it would be for him to be there instead of the Sigs Building. He bought it and we really didn't see much of him for a while. At first things were pretty slow and we took turns of working every second day, but being on call if one or the other needed a hand. At least until things got busy again.

When I put in my release I met with an officer who I hadn't met before and he was telling me what a great career I had and such and that he wished me good luck. I was certainly thinking, "Oh go fuck yourself."

Shortly after the return to Canada I applied for school at the National Institute of Broadcasting in Winnipeg and started night school and only told a few people initially. I was two or three months into my degree when the Battalion got back up and running again with the rest of the troops.

To say the least, there was a massive change in the Battalion. Some troops either stayed in Germany changing to different trades, or got married and got out of the military and stayed in Germany, or got back to Canada and changed trades or got out all together like I did. The rest remained with the Battalion, but it was quite the turnover and they were sure fast tracking people out.

I did do one final exercise in Shilo, where the base is now in fact, and knew I'd likely miss some school, but no matter, I was still in the army. Well our WO Ron knew I was going to school and he didn't want me to miss class, so he let me use a jeep twice a week to get back for school in Winnipeg and then back the next day to Shilo to the exercise. It was a classy thing to do. Oh and if you remember the story of the WO I shook up and threw to the ground, well that's who it was, Ron Cameron. He was a good man to me. I made an effort in the summer of 2017 to stop up and see him in Bissett Manitoba as that's where he retired and that is also where I used to camp as a kid.

30-years later - I didn't mean to throw you. Was just kidding

It was really good to see him and to catch up a bit. He was a changed man from the Bosnia tour though, as were many of the boys who had to struggle through with the lovely UN in charge of that disaster. It was good to catch up if only for a short while.

The final exercise I did was really a holiday, Adventure Training in Minaki Ontario with the Sigs crew. Living in the woods of course, but it was really camping and fishing. Who'd have thought, it only took over eight years for the Recruiters words to come through. Rick Turner and Ron Cameron were in charge of us and it was a fun relaxing week or so. I was pretty much done after that.

I was at a get together somewhere on base before leaving and a Major I didn't like, I should include, almost no one liked, decided to spill his drink on me on purpose and thought it was pretty funny. He however didn't think it was funny when I threw my drink in his face. Go figure. I didn't care he was a prick anyway. He told me he would get me before I got out, but didn't.

So once the decision was made to get out I was as ready in my mind as I could be. I had someone tell me I'd never make it on Civvy Street. I wasn't the first one told that either. I swore I wouldn't go back in the army to prove him wrong. As I wasn't in for ten years there wasn't much of a pension, though I would get my contributions back, and I opted for the cash out lump sum payment as I didn't want much to do with the military and have them somehow screw up my monthly pension. As it was, it took damn near six months to get the funds.

With Honor

I worked with some great people over the years, through a lot of crap. Had some good leaders as well, including officers. I was harder on them in this story because the bad ones could do the most damage to a career, and some did to mine. But there were some damn fine Officers I worked for as well.

So after doing all the things I have spoken about, learned to live in the harshest places you can think of in the worst conditions, surviving with or without, not being around much, being trained to kill or defend myself, taking orders, learning we are only as strong as our weakest man, being prepared for many things just in case, to drift someone to settle a dispute, saying what I truly thought, teamwork and the true meaning of brothers and honor, really none of that prepared me for Civvy Street.

And don't worry the release medical says you are perfectly healthy

Oh, and while you are out there, hey make sure you act normal like everyone else.

It was then, when I hit Civvy Street that I truly realized I just wasn't the same anymore.

Memories

CHAPTER 8

Well here I come. Hello Civvyland-1989-Present

Well shit, that wasn't what I was expecting. I was still going to night school when I first got out and I likely did what most military guys do when they got out. I didn't get a haircut, grew the mullet and didn't shave very often. When it was cold, I just went in the house. Creature comforts that didn't include modular tents. We didn't get that freedom or choice in the army for sure. I was even on pogey for the first time in my life. Some may remember those days in the late 80's where you had to bring in these cards to the unemployment office every two weeks and wait to get paid, while the cheques never ever came on time or when you needed it. There was no direct deposit in those days and I hated it with a passion.

I even had to go to a couple of interviews with some official from the office. They could be power trippers for sure. My first visit was basically to get set up, but then they called me for a second interview to talk about my job options. This was my first interesting civvy conversation since I got out.

"What job options? I'm going to school for my job options."

"Mr. Okrainec you have to go for three job interviews each pay period or we'll place you in one."

"Well you can place me into whatever job you want but I won't show up."

"Well you have to or we'll cut you off."

"Listen, I paid into this ever since I started working and I am entitled to the benefits. I'm not screwing you. I got out of the army to get into the media, I'm bloody well going to school just for that, so really you can go fuck yourself, I need to see the next person up the chain here."

The Manager came later and agreed with my story and didn't cut me off, but told me not a good idea to tell the guy who would give me funds to go fuck himself.

Well roger that I suppose, but I never did get payments on time and swore, if possible, I would never ever go on pogey again. I didn't like being treated like a mooch, even though I paid into this benefit each paycheque. Fortunately, to date, I haven't had to go back.

After about four months, while still waiting for my pension payout of course, I decided I needed to do something and ended up with my first job since getting out. I was just about done school and had no idea what the future held at that point, other than the time came where I needed a haircut, likely had to shave and was close to running out of field pay.

So, as this was really the start of my civvy life and experiences, I should touch on just what jobs I did have over the many years since I got out, as the stories and situations I ran into are part of this story.

So as a thumbnail version this is where work life has taken me on Civvy Street. I was a Sportscaster for a couple of years in Brandon, which is what I really wanted to do, went over to the Fairs and Exhibitions Industry for close to a decade, both in Brandon and Yorkton, Saskatchewan and now close to two decades in the Real Estate Industry Managing Shopping Centre's In Yorkton, Winnipeg and Medicine Hat. Real Estate will likely be where I'll retire from when the time comes.

Over the years a common talking point I have heard from vets who were starting over and working in their new lives on Civvy Street was, they just did their job. They got traction by just doing their job. None of them, me included, did something really special. Just worried about the task at hand, as that's all we can control anyway, and just do your job. This is not advice to anyone, just a fact.

And so it began. I scanned through the paper to see what options there were and ended up applying at the European Health Spa. They were the Goodlife Fitness of the 80's and 90's. I had to even put together my first resume. That was interesting as well as just what the hell does and ex-military guy put on a resume after coming out of the Army. That I was a decent shot, that I could use a compass, that I knew how to insert a bayonet into someone, that I could work in the worst environment possible, that I could eat anything or if someone was bothering anyone in the office that I could drift them or take them out. Ummm…no, I guess I had had to put down some other info.

The day after I applied I got an interview and was offered the job starting the next day. It wasn't rocket science for sure. We put people through workouts, I got to go to work in gym clothes, and had the opportunity to work out as well. The pay was minimum wage but the paycheque could be quite decent with commissions if any of the various membership packages were sold to a client. The more I sold the more I made.

Well I was pretty sure I could handle that. I showed up my first day and did what was required. The day was slow for people as far as customers, so I started making cold calls to sell memberships, while also keeping busy taking people through workouts. It was just my luck the owner was up in Winnipeg from somewhere in the States. He was a good guy, liked vets and was a bodybuilder. He was pretty ripped. We started shooting the shit and hit it off right away and at the end of my first day, he promoted me to Manager. He gave me the opportunity to run one of the gyms that was struggling for memberships, which turned out, was for a few months. Well, all on my first day.

Well shit, this civvy thing was easy. Mostly it was just doing my job and showing some initiative that got me noticed. So now I am still pretty young, still gung-ho and I got to workout all day, if I wanted. The job was twelve hour days, three days a week as back then they had guy days and ladies days. Spandex had just become popular, the yoga pants back then, so ummm…sometimes I had paperwork to do on my off days. The difference as manager was I received commissions on what the staff sold as well. I didn't really get paid a ton but liked the job none the less and it was something to do.

The job was alright in the short term, but too much infighting between the various Managers which I wasn't into. The jest was to run the building, which had a pretty large gym, a pool, a sauna, along with all the various weights and fitness machines. Of course when I took over I was a hardass and actually made people bring their membership cards in to prove they were actually members. Some of them didn't come back and I wondered just how long they worked out for free without being a member. I also gave a shit about the place, which was a dirty mess and cleaned it all up. When the boss came to visit he thought it was a new place.

Over my short time there I saw quite a few body builders train as they prepared for the Mr. Manitoba Contest. I didn't know people could grow muscles in some of the places they did. Then again, they certainly weren't built like Johnny from the competition in Germany.

During my stay at the spa I also kept my focus as to the reason I got out of the military, to get into the media. So when I had some time off I still managed to drive the TransCanada from Manitoba to BC dropping off demo tapes to all the radio and TV stations along the way. I wanted to stay on track. I also finally got my pension contributions which gave me some breathing room. Well other than the fact they put it all into RRSP's, which I had no idea what that was back then or what the tax implications would be. I had to withdraw most of it to get by, pay off some debts and paid for it dearly the next tax year. Where's my fuckin field pay?

After three or four months working at the Spa I finally got the call, and my break so to speak, and was offered a weekend news and sports gig as a Country Station in Brandon. It was the most popular station in the area.

I gave my notice at the spa and the owner was bummed but understood. I noticed the place closed down not long after as the spa's started to close throughout Canada, so my timing was good.

Now, I was from Manitoba, but had never been to Brandon before, other than passing by on the TransCanada. The job was only weekends, but it was the start I was looking for and needed the old foot in the door. I made the trip each weekend from Winnipeg for a whole $5.00 an hour, which was minimum wage at the time. Well in Cyprus that got a few drinks, but that money didn't buy much in Canada and I felt like a poor private all over again. That part sucked. I was still entitled to a portion of pogey until I was full time, so helped a bit, but of course the cheque still never came on time.

Now when I started this project I wanted to tell some stories and situations I have encountered as an Army guy in the world of Civvies. Hopefully when you read some of what I came up against, that those of you struggling to find your place may have some hope, because if I can do it so can you. There is no right or wrong, only how I did it. It wasn't easy. It still isn't easy. The thing is you have to want to. I left the army, but the army didn't leave me. Despite how pissed off I was back when I got out, the PPCLI made me what I am today, along with my parents of course. I am still that up front don't ask me something if you don't want the truth who still runs into many "Go fuck yourself moments," it's just that I pick my spots more.

Oh this life hasn't been easy and I am surprised through all these years I haven't beat the shit out of someone, though I have come close and have been talked down by a boss or two before it got that far. When you see some of the instances, well some of you likely would have felt like drifting someone to. But really as we mature or gain some experience I just try to keep true to my values and solve the problems in other ways. This posed challenges however, especially while working a stretch in the Corporate World where it seems companies care more about shareholders and not as much about staff. It's a difficult world to function in, especially the way I am.

Now back when I just got out as a young ex-army guy my reading consisted of the sports page and the comics. I didn't care about news or current events, politics or opinion pieces or really anything like that. But times changed and I started showing much interest in many other things, especially local and federal politics and community groups.

Through all the "Go fuck yourselves" along the way I managed to become a Chamber of Commerce President, in Yorkton, President of Saskatchewan Fairs, President of the local competitive Soccer Club, a term as a City Councillor and sat on many many boards and committees. Looking back at all the previous stories I noted from my Army days, well who would have thought I would have done this. I just felt giving back to the community, wherever I was, was important. For me it was time to quit bitching about how things were going or disagreeing with how things were done and put my money where my mouth was and try to become part of the solution, whatever it was. Somewhere along the line I just wanted to help make a difference, in a community kind of way. Don't worry along the way I messed up, but really feel I did some good too.

So in the army pretty much everything we did was teamwork and we were only as strong as our weakest man, but most importantly we just did our job. Some places I've worked have been like that, but certainly not as common especially from where I was coming from. We actually believed this and worked like it in the military.

I should also get this part out of the way. The biggest challenge I had at first was working with women. Not because of gender issues or that I was a he-man or anything like that, but you need to understand in the army I was in, there were no women that we worked with, or rarely. There were in other trades, but as far as our Battalion, we had 0, nada. The ones I got to know in the military, especially in Germany, more or less spoke like we did, so it was just part of our life.

So naturally all our greetings were "Morning Cocksucker", "Hey Asswipe", "You stupid fuck" and that was the polite version. That was just normal army talk every day for over eight years. Well to say the least some of this language and sayings didn't go over well at the start of my new careers. Go figure.

So one day early in my transition we were having a staff meeting. The crew I was working with was a mixture of men and women and most of us were friends. So the staff meeting was moving along and my female friend was talking to the boss and kind of brown nosing a bit. So I looked at her and said, "Ok that's enough you bag licker." Well shit, the tears started to flow and she said I could use a better choice of words. Too me that comment was normal and it was how we talked every minute of every day. Well turns out it this wasn't normal in this world.

So HR called me in his office, my boss, and said that I needed to clean it up a lot. You think!!!

Of course I spoke with her after, she was my friend, and apologised to let her know it wasn't her, just the way I always talked. It was really then I realized I wasn't in the army any more. Well fuck, I needed to clean it up a lot (but not completely). Dumbfuck

I have had many female bosses over my time in my other careers, some really good and some really bad, and really in the end not much different than men, some good bosses, some bad. The only difference was you could drift the men in the face if you were pissed off.

My part time job in Radio doing weekend news and sports went well enough that I was offered the job full time. I was still covering some news, but mostly it was sports, all for the honor of making $11,000 a year. Cripes, the pay was like being a poor private again, without the camping, hunting, fishing and money in the bank. Man, I kept thinking, "Where's my field pay!!!" Money wise those years were tough.

I just kept going back to, "You're not going to make it on Civvy Street Okrainec."

Most of us got along in the newsroom, likely because we were all making the same crappy money and just trying to start our careers. The younger staff anyway. Also, being in the media wasn't all the glory you may think it is or what you may hear or even see on TV. There was much work and travel before the stories made it on the air.

While many of us got along there was still the issue of dealing with some massive egos in this business. I suppose in some cases an ego was required to get ahead in the business. There sure were some swelled heads. I kept thinking, "Christ, you are at a country station in Brandon, not fucking Hollywood."

As for me, well there weren't many sports that happened during the day, so there was lots of evening work attending games, doing interviews, preparing stories for air and so on. My days off were Monday's and Tuesday's, but I still had to work one of those days prepping stories for whatever league I was covering. The timing of the work never bothered me. I mean I had many worse hours in the Army for sure, and I didn't have to wiggle my toes to make sure they wouldn't be pulled off.

Despite the pay, I really liked the job. It's what kept me going. I got to cover a lot of sports, meet many young people who were trying to make it to the bigs, good coaches and even better competition. I started in the fall, so covered the local High School Football league and Brandon University Sports. This included Men's and Ladies Basketball and the Men's Hockey team. The Bobcat Men's Basketball Team was four time National Champions when I was there. It was hard not to like the Basketball for sure. This was an awesome team with loud and crazy fans.

I was also assigned the Manitoba Junior Hockey League, AAA Midget Hockey, Baseball Leagues, All-Star games and many others. My main beat in the winter was the University, the MJHL (Manitoba Junior Hockey League) and Triple A Midget Hockey. I had the opportunity to do play by play and color commentary on air for games for various sports. If you think doing play by play of say a hockey game is easy, try it. It takes practise. You have to learn every player and call the game on the fly. Once you learn and get some practise it's a lot of fun, even if I called the wrong player on the fly at times. I covered it all if it was in our area, travelled and also had weekly reports to put together. My boss mainly did the Wheat Kings Hockey and more of the larger events that were around at the time. I travelled a lot around the province to many small towns and cities. I was also part of the World Curling Championships, the Canadian Men's and Ladies Curling Championships, the World Youth Baseball Championships among the many other events. I certainly was in my element.

I remember doing some of the PA announcing at the World Youth Baseball Tournament. There were teams from all over the world, but the names from Chinese Taipei and Korea were, to say the least, challenging. Some of the batters, after I announced they were coming to bat, would be just shaking their heads, probably thinking what the hell, whose name is he saying. All you could do is laugh. I certainly wasn't a professional.

News and sports consisted of reporting events and games of course, but also about getting the scoop before the other stations and the dreaded sources you have heard about. I wasn't big on sources and anonymous tips and such, but sometimes it was handy. Our station was by far the most listened to in the area at the time, so certainly what was reported people heard. They had a very large following and because we got around to so many places people knew who we were. I also learned that when reporting something, especially if it was a negative story, that I best have the facts straight before going to air with it, because if it was the wrong information it could be curtains for the job.

This coincidently came to a head for me one winter. I did a story on a particular coach, who, to say the least, could be quite difficult. He got into an altercation with fans in the lobby of a hockey rink one night, I wasn't there, but it was my beat of one of the leagues I was tasked to cover. So I did my investigation and interviews with various people and went to air with the story.

Well the next day it was a big issue at the station. When I came in to work I was getting strange looks and no one was talking to me. WTF, I was the hot gossip of the day. Well HR, the Station boss and the News Director let me know the coach I did the report on was the husband of one of the staff members who were entrenched at the station. She was pissed to say the least. She let them know I was ruining his career and certainly lobbied for me to be fired.

So I'm thinking, wouldn't the cause of his perceived career decline be the result of the fact that he was in a fucking fight in the lobby of a hockey rink, but you know, maybe that's just me. Through it all I found out that all the Station Manager wanted to know was if story was in fact, true. They checked into it and my story was in fact true and that was the end of it. But I was certainly careful eating muffins in the coffee room after that. Then again I was ex-army and probably would have survived a poisoning. Shit if I could eat army rations dated back to the Vietnam War, I could pretty much eat anything.

What I did learn though, was that even if the story was true, just how quick, if you really wanted to, you could ruin someone's life or reputation. But being in this job I couldn't pick favorites either.

As media we also got invited too many events, either as a thanks, or to help promote whatever the event was. One day I was at the station and a Police Officer came in and they asked if there was someone from the station who would like to take part in the RCMP's Canadian Pistol Shoot Competition taking place in Brandon.

Well in the army I learned never (well mostly never) to volunteer, but I was all over this and I got to take part in the competition. Now these target pistols were better than the 9mm pistols we used in the army. This was because the pistol barrel was a bit longer and easier to aim. I hadn't done any shooting for a while and saw my first two shots were just outside the bulls-eye and I walked the rest of my shots in closer to the center. When I was finished and brought my target in, and ended up winning the competition. The one RCMP who was beside me said to someone that he coached me as to how to aim and shoot, but I called bullshit and let them know I was ex-army and had fired a couple rounds in my life. Was pretty cool, beating them all, and I kept that target for a long time, along with my winning plaque.

Beat them police dudes

I was pretty close in my dealings with the Brandon Wheat Kings in those days, mostly because I was always in the arena during the winter. But back then they were not a very good hockey team. Also, being teenagers for the most part, sometimes they got into trouble. Read Mcpl Okrainec, army version. Well one day one of the kids was in police trouble. It was my bosses beat, but he was out on the road, so instead of doing a story I called up the GM/Coach, who I knew fairly well, and asked how he was doing. I also let him know that I in fact wasn't doing a story, just concerned about the kid. To me he was just young and I didn't want to go there. An adult should know better. I know 100% for sure my boss would have run the story. I got the scoop, made sure he was ok and I know Kelly appreciated me not doing a story that went to air about the incident. Sometimes a guy had to have limits.

By the second year at the station I got a massive raise to $12,000. At this rate I would only need to work another thirty years to make a comfortable living. It really sucked, but I truly loved what I did, the people I met, some famous, some not. I was never awestruck with someone who was pretty famous, to me people were people.

So things were going fine, other than the money, and I branched out and also became more comfortable in writing as well. I started doing some freelance on the side with a local newspaper twice a week, and also created a monthly newsletter for the University. It was a bit of extra money and I really enjoyed the writing.

The News Director wasn't happy though. Apparently I wasn't allowed to make some extra money to eat. He was a horrible, backstabbing weasel of a boss. We rarely saw him and the only one he looked after was himself. I kept doing the writing though, so he was on my back more.

Well, once I started writing on the side it was just a matter of time until the reckoning came. You see my sports boss used to like pulling pranks. He loved them, as long as there weren't any against him. He pulled a few on me like leaving a message that I had to call IP Nightly and stupid shit like that. You'd call not paying attention, look like an idiot and knew you'd been had.

Finally as revenge, he was on the road with the Wheat Kings and he called in to record his report for me to be included with the morning the news and sportscast. After he did his report he was waiting for the night DJ to pick the phone back up and make sure the report went through, and the DJ was busy for a while. While he was waiting he was singing to himself and it was all recorded. So naturally that's how I lead off my sportscast the next morning. I let him showcase his talents in the background while I read the sports to roughly 100-150,000 listeners.

Well, to say the least, he was livid and whined endlessly to the News Director as I cracked some of his ego I suppose. The HR Department (News Director) gave me the spiel about labour laws and apparently I wasn't allowed to do this for all our listeners. I was suddenly not suitable for the position and was laid off shortly after. Prick. So it didn't matter how hard I worked, for no money, I wasn't allowed payback to those who were my boss. It didn't matter that it was done to many of us in reverse. Talk about thin skin. But that's how egos can work. This wasn't like the world I was coming from or was used to. This sports guy is now on TSN and I often wondered how many people he stabbed in the back to get there. As for the News Director, it took a while, but he was eventually fired, but how many careers did he ruin along the way. There was quite a few just in the two years I was there.

"You're not going to make it on Civvy Street Okrainec." Remembering this just made me dig in more.

In the end, when in the media, if any of us wanted to get ahead we had to move to bigger and bigger markets, which meant moving a lot. Well I had enough of that for a while and getting laid off ended up being a good thing, but certainly I was still pissed. I had given up a career to give this a try and egos and thin skin put an end to that, there anyway. Then again quite a few of my mates got laid off in the short times they were there as well. Guess they didn't want anyone getting to that magic $13,000 mark from the news room. For me it was all the coaches and athletes I missed. There were certainly some really good folks around that end of the province.

A few years later I was in Toronto for a convention and did what any good Canadian would do, headed over to the Hockey Hall of Fame. Pretty damn awesome place. So later I was going through the Souvenir Shop looking for something Winnipeg Jets, like a watch, and someone tapped me on the shoulder and asks if I was Richard Okrainec. I said, "Ya." He let me know he was the GM of the Southwest Cougars from the Triple A Midget Hockey League, which was my old beat. I was really close with that team and the Midget Wheat Kings. He said to me, "I never got a chance to just say thanks for all the work you did covering the league." And also thanked me for everything I did for their team as well. They missed having me around and just having one person say thanks made it all worth it.

That compliment was pretty cool, and unexpected, especially while cruising the Hockey Hall of Fame. It's the little things that make life good and certainly I felt a lot better.

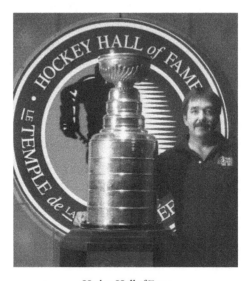

Hockey Hall of Fame

If you can imagine, I did manage for two years and all that time on the air, to never once swear on a live broadcast. Coming from the army, that was one of my biggest successes for sure.

I, of course, also continued to play sports, at least until the body started breaking down. Fastball and broomball mainly, which included some serious teams and some fun teams. Later, after not playing anything for a few years, I eventually got into playing soccer. I played a little in the army but not like this. I was the old dude at 36 at this point in my life. Well the team had pretty much everyone younger than me including teenagers. It was hard keeping up when I became the old dog. At first we weren't very good, but within a couple years became one of the best teams in the Province. We won a lot of tournaments no matter the level. I stuck with it until I was 40, then it became a bit too hard on the joints. The following year, after I was done, the team won Premier League Provincials and went to Nationals. We had some really great players from all the soccer nations. Christ man, I had injuries in that sport though. We played indoor and outdoor soccer. Torn hamstrings, concussions, dislocated thumb, pulled calves, you name it. Had some good times and stories of course. Just finally got too old and started coaching kids instead.

Any way back to life on Civvy Street, as for me I just plowed ahead.

I wasn't unemployed very long and a short time later I got a good job as the Media Coordinator with the Exhibition Association in Brandon. This is an organization who puts together various annual fairs and events including Summer Fairs, Ag Shows, major Horse Shows including equestrian and heavy horse, Pro Rodeo's and many others. It was an event based business with many a long hours of preparation, lots of meetings, organization and set up.

I also stayed involved with the Wheat Kings, who were located in the same building I worked in, the Keystone Centre, and I did Color Commentary for their games and went on the road when I got a chance and wasn't working. It was a great way to get to know some of the players on those long bus rides. Like I said, in those days they weren't very good. Some of them made it to the NHL though. One is even the GM of the Jets. I once went a year doing 34 losses in a row. They had won some on the road but I wasn't there because of work commitments. They however started turning things around, after the few years of struggling, when Kelly McCrimmon took over and have been a contender for many many years. It was painful though being a fan in those days.

I ended up in the Fair business for about decade, first in Brandon, then later in Yorkton. I remember not long after moving to Saskatchewan in 1995 I started getting messages from army buddies asking how I liked living in The Gap. I didn't know what The Gap was, but it turned out to be the space between Manitoba and Alberta. I used to ride the Saskatchewan boys hard in the army, being a Manitoba boy, so it was payback time for them. Ha, I deserved it. Who would have thought a hard core Blue Bomber fan would end up in the heart of Rider Nation for about twenty years. What made it worse was the fact that not long after moving there the Bombers weren't very good for a long time. Well that was bad timing for sure. Most in Rider nation who knew me gave it to me on a regular basis. Those buggers, but all in good fun, even against those Banjo Picking Inbreds.

Here's just one quick story of Rider Nation vs Blue Bombers. One day living in Yorkton, my neighbour was naturally a major fan in Rider nation. Everyone who knew me knew I was blue through and through. One night I came home to a large sign on my living room window noting I was the, "Number 1 Rider Fan" and there were also signs all over my fence that said, "I love the Riders." So, later that evening I noticed they were in their back yard with company. I quietly went to my shed, pulled out the mower, put the wheels to the lowest setting and went to their plush front yard and cut a huge WPG across their nice front lawn. They never heard me and I just carried on after that. Well they didn't notice until they came home from work the next day, and there was no getting that out until the grass grew back. The lawyer husband wasn't happy and I heard him chewing out his wife, who put the signs up in my yard. Payback is a bitch. I didn't get any more signs after that though.

As time went on in Brandon the Media Coordinator grew into Operations, which was something I was familiar with from my Sigs days, and eventually to Manager in Yorkton. Mainly this was because of hard work, but mostly just doing my job. People often asked if the job was full time. Ha, it was that plus, as anyone who may have worked in that business would know. Events just don't show up. So much work is put into planning.

In Brandon there where around eight full-time staff who worked for a Board of Directors of fifty. In Yorkton there were two of us full time who worked for a Board of twenty five. So Directors, in a sense were also our boss, and we hired more staff when the actual events came up. The planning of events was much work and meetings, especially when the events were quickly approaching. When the events were on it was very long hours, in early, home late. There were also many varying opinions and socializing as well. It really was a lot of work and coordination getting a five acre building (in Brandon) ready for all the various events which took place during the course of the shows.

Naturally at times I had HR issues, which usually were dealt with by my boss or one of the executives. We all worked hard in that industry, thankless many times, but I enjoyed it. There was lots of action and we had to be prepared for anything. The Boards were made up of volunteers who put in a lot of work on their own time. They were really committed to their particular event, and for the most part great people.

One of the events we had in Brandon was the Bud Pro Rodeo Series. We were one of the stops on this Pro Tour which was broadcast on CBC. Many of the top Rodeo Contestants from around North America came, as it was big prize money, while the stop was also part of the points system to get to the National Finals in Vegas. Many of these cowboys and cowgirls also competed at the Canadian Finals in Edmonton, should they make it. They were the true Pro's on the North American Circuit. Bull Riding, Bareback, Saddle Bronc, Steer Wrestling, Calf Roping, Barrel Racing, all the major Rodeo events.

Now all of the events were awesome, if you were into Rodeo, but the Bull Riding was crazy. You had to be some committed to get on that massive animal that wanted you off, and if bucked off then would try to trample or gore the rider. The Rodeo Clowns played such a huge roll in distracting the animals when a rider was in trouble, while also entertaining the crowd in between.

I also learned it may not be a good idea to pick a fight with a Bull Rider. One night in the Bull Riding Competition I saw one guy, Ted Nuce I believe his name was, getting the rough ride of his life. He got hung up and knocked out cold from the Bulls head and bucked off, but his hand was caught. So he was flipped around like a rag doll until his hand finally got free and he fell to the ground out cold. Then, the bull chucked him around some more. It was nuts.

He was taken away in an ambulance and I was wondering if he'd even survive. A few hours later I saw him in our bar pounding beers and two weeks later he won the big prize in Vegas. I wonder what all them cowboy bones and joints feel like when they get older. Tough bastards.

During one of the Rodeo's we also had the protesters roll in. Now you can feel how you want about Rodeo, but if you are coming to an agricultural town to tell them how they should live, well, that's not a good idea. So of course they snuck down to the arena, gathered quickly in the main area, got a sign up, and handcuffed themselves to the fence. Of course the Rodeo Contestants and much of the crowd didn't like them. So they bucked a horse, steered it over to where they were and the cowboy bucked off and kicked one of them square in the jaw. Once we finally got bolt cutters and cut the cuffs, they refused to walk, so we had to drag them up the stairs through the crowd to get them out. Bad idea there too, as people were coming out of the crowd and drifting them in the face. I'm not sure how they felt about their protest, but I know their jaws didn't feel very good.

While with the Exhibition in Brandon I was working out of the Keystone Centre. It was a massive building of 5 acres, even bigger now, so you had events everywhere in there, thus why the planning and set up had to be so organized. It was a big place to put together for the events.

So one day I was outside heading to our shop and looked over and seen an MLVW and a bunch of troops parked over in the shade. I walked over and low and behold it was some of the boys from 2PPLCI chowing down from those awesome hay box lunches I used to enjoy....not. I looked around and there was Rick Lawler. He was the guy who got me promoted, and one of the good guys. Well holy fuck!! I hadn't seen him in quite some time. So of course he did the right thing and got me a melmac plate and cup and gave me some lunch. I was reminded why a man cannot live on army food alone. I jest, as it wasn't that bad and it was good to see some of the brothers on their way to wherever they were going, and to get my monthly fill of f...bombs for about an hour or so.

Working at this job was good for me as I really had to be self-motivated, give a shit about the department I worked in, to work pretty much unsupervised, and be very organized. Just do your job. Very much, in the work sense, an army structure, so I was good at it. It was also similar to what I used to do and we all got to see what people were like when a crisis hit. Obviously the term crisis was different in the army, but in this industry we all had to adapt when things didn't go as planned. Being as this was an event based business and we were putting together dozens upon dozens of events and activities, things were bound to go south eventually. We also had to work a lot with the public as they paid to come to the events, but holy crap some of them you just couldn't please.

Some days you knew you were doomed for bad luck. A perfect example was one fair in Yorkton. I had hired quite a few part time staff for the set up and tear down of the many events. Shortly before the start of the show, like within a half an hour of opening to the public, one of the boys came in and let me know one of the staff had broken their ankle hanging up the "Watch Your Step" sign. How bloody ironic. He was hanging the sign, standing on a chair, stepped off wrong and broke his ankle. Well so much for health and safety I suppose.

Dealing with the Directors was mostly good, I mean come on, they weren't getting paid, they just did it because they loved the industry or whatever particular event they were in charge of, all while putting in mega hours on their own, just to support their community. Talk about thankless at times, and I can say without a doubt, these events would never have been successful without them. There was every walk of life on the boards from business people to farmers. They got paid in thanks, meals and drinks, and of course the success of their particular event.

And man we used to prank each other, without the worry of getting laid off by people with thin skin like the media days. You had to have fun in this job.

One time the boss went away for meetings and when he came back we had tied all of his furniture to the ceiling. The desks, chairs, cabinets, bookshelves, the whole lot. Another time he came back to a barnyard of chickens clucking in his office. At another event we had an accountant who kept stealing the cans for his recycling, so we set him up by gluing them down and then watched him as he tried to pick them up getting frustrating why they were stuck.

I worked with a Director who was a big man who had a heart of gold. What he also had was a big appetite and he was there to work and eat. He liked his food. One event that was put together was a massive community steak night. One Director came in and asked him how the steaks were and his reply was, "Well, the first two were pretty tough, but the third one was ok."

They liked to have fun, but also had times when they just wanted their way. At one event I'd set up one of our concerts with Patricia Conroy and Blue Rodeo. I had scheduled Blue Rodeo play the first two sets and was finishing up the concert with Conroy, who was big on the country scene at the time. So that meant she wouldn't be going on the stage early enough for one of the Directors and he wanted her to play first before he left. So he said to me,

"Richard, you get Conroy on that stage right now or I'm walking out that door."

So naturally I replied,

"Well first before you go can you leave me your drink tickets and don't let the door hit your ass on the way out."

Another Director over heard me and spit his beer out his nose.

So, of course, the next day the HR Department had me in the office and told me it probably wasn't a good idea to talk to the Vice President like that. And I didn't get the drink tickets either. Everyone got over it pretty quick.

Another time when I was Manager I had a Director in my office going on and on about another Director. "He an asshole," "I can't work with him," etc. etc. As perfect timing would have it, the Director he was talking about walked by my office. I just said, "Hold that thought," and walked out to the office and asked him to come in. I then looked at the Director and said, "Ok, now tell him what you just told me." He just looked at me stunned. Well I didn't make a friend, but the issue went away when he wouldn't say it to his face. Funny how that works.

Trade shows were a big part of all the events as well. There were hundreds of booths who did the Fair circuit through various times of the year, selling pretty much anything you want. At every Fair there was usually a Military Recruiting booth. I would always go over to chat while also hoping one day it would be someone I knew. So wouldn't you know it on one of these days, now many years after I got out, and who walks into my office but my good buddy Alden Friesen. Who would have thought that big bastard would be recruiting. I bet he still used the same lines to convince potential recruits that everything was light in the PPCLI.

After picking my jaw up off the desk, I really didn't get a lot of work done the rest of the day visiting. Later upstairs at the Exhibitor Reception, while having some drinks of course, he tells the local Reserve Officers that I'm an ex-Patricia (well always a Patricia) and from there they were on me like white on rice the rest of the night to join. They were good guys but I told them to bugger off because it just wasn't happening and joked I didn't like Officers anyway. Fuckin Alden. Was good to see him as at that point it had been many years, but really that's how it is with all of us. Just catch up like we were never apart.

In Brandon the biggest event was the Royal Manitoba Winter Fair. This was a six day event with the main feature being Equestrian and Heavy Horse Shows, which drew about 200,000 people each year. It was a good event and certainly our most popular. So one year at the kickoff breakfast I got the call that labor was in progress for my first child. So I spent the better part of the six days between the hospital and the fair and ran the Media Room from the Waiting Room. I didn't miss a beat. My boss never forgot that and even used that story as my reference when applied for the Manager's Job in Yorkton.

It was a boy, Matthew, and a pretty famous baby in those parts, as I did most of the media interviews for our organization and when I was around all of the interviews were about him and not the fair. Years later the Directors still asked how the winter fair baby was doing.

I often joked, as I was there for the birth, that when he came out I said, "Holy crap he's hung like a horse," from which the nurse replied, "Ummm that's the umbilical cord Mr. Okrainec." My daughter Samantha was also born in Brandon, though not during the Fair.

My old boss did like the way I worked but sometimes I would plough through tasks with carnage just to get it done. I didn't really like the sit around and wait for the decision process when the job could already be done. I heard him tell another Director that he looked at me as someone who could take the hill, but on the way there would be casualties. I always felt some people's feelings just got hurt to quick and there were times I just couldn't wait as I had a million other things to do. I got over it and the work always got done.

Eventually the Manager's job opened up in Brandon and a couple of us who worked in the office, applied. We were both interviewed but neither got the position. They ended up hiring from outside the organization, likely because the other guy had more business experience, and I really couldn't argue with that. I had overheard my boss speaking with the other guy from the office prior to our interviews about when he got the job, so I called one of the Directors and just said, "If I am just getting a courtesy interview I will just save everyone the time." He indicated the interview wasn't like that and I believed him. But one Director told me I was too young and not ready for the position. Who knows if they were right, but age shouldn't matter.

I wasn't bitter, but another opportunity came about shortly after, when I saw the Manager position in Yorkton opened up. Yorkton was a smaller city and fair, but many of the same type of events we were doing. I overheard some Directors talking that I wouldn't get that one either, and it was sure starting to sound familiar. In any event I applied and made the trip out there for the interview. This was the first time I was in Yorkton. It turned out I was the only out of towner they interviewed, I blew them away in my interview and eventually I got the job. The head hunter told me after, it was one of the best interviews he was involved in. Well I did know what I was talking about and had lots of ideas that I never got the opportunity to implement. It was tough for them to hire me though, as it would be hard to say no to someone local that they knew.

In the end for me it wasn't about the money, though the pay was much better than those radio days. It was about the opportunity really, for the first time since I got out of the Military, to lead in a meaningful way. They eventually relented, offered me the position, and it was off to another place where I hadn't been and didn't know anyone, other than one guy who I knew through the Fair Industry, and start again.

But mainly it was about, "You're not going to make it on Civvy Street Okrainec."

I guess the real big difference between the Army and Civvy Street was the fact that when posted in the Army, you were going with many people you knew. On Civvy Street you are on your own. But I was, and still am, a believer that every place is what you make it, so I never whined about it.

The Exhibition in Yorkton had lots of potential, and it was a great small city to raise kids. I never looked back.

When I arrived my bosses were the President and the Executive of the Board. My first President was exactly like me and we told each other to "Go Fuck Yourself," a few times. He was a really good guy and we are still friends. The next President, as they did two year terms, was an accountant and he really taught me a lot as well from the business side of things and also helped me develop to be a bit more polished and professional. Both of them had different styles and I always appreciated what they did for me.

It was here that I decided if I was to be the face of a high profile community organization I'd likely have to change my ways a bit, not completely, but I couldn't always say the first go to thought in my head. It wasn't always easy for sure, when I have been that way most of my life, but hey I tried for the most part.

What they also forgot to tell me as part of the interview was the organization was $250K in debt and struggling to raise revenues. The money making events were paying for those events that were losing money. It wasn't anything sinister, just what organizations such as theirs were going through, especially for the agricultural events.

Well I had a whirlwind of ideas in my head which I pitched to the Board, they liked the ideas, many of which I learned from my Brandon days, along with other ideas from my warped mind. The biggest one was implementing a large sponsorship program which they certainly did not have in place at that time. An example would be, say a large community business was a $100 sponsor of some event or show, and I noted I bet I could get $5,000 instead, not just with one business, but many of them. I would build a sponsor package to something they would be interested in so they could either decide locally or get approval from their corporate entity.

Well I was proud of the fact that after the four plus years I was the Manager, that when I left the organization was debt free, with money in the bank (like the army eh). The sponsorship program was hugely successful and went from about $8-10K per year to over $100K in annual revenue. The start of the success wasn't all because of the sponsorship, as we overall changed how we did things and for the most part presented events people wanted to go to.

As a result of the improvements we made, we were rewarded at the Canadian Fair Convention the next year, winning Canada's Regional Fair of the Year, for our Summer Fair. I was also nominated as a finalist for Canada's Fair Manager of the Year. All three of us Finalists were friends, one from Saskatchewan and the other from Alberta, and the nomination was something I was proud of and being in that group with all of my peers in Canada there. Grace from Alberta won, and I'm still bitter about it Grace. You hag!! Just kidding, she deserved it for sure. Glen, the other finalist and I bugged her for quite some time about it. All in all it was a good year for us.

Over my years in the Fair Business I made it to the Conventions in Halifax, London, Winnipeg, Calgary, Saskatoon and Toronto. I also got to see just how other Fairs, of all sizes, did things, which was always helpful. This is where we found that many of them had the same problems as us and that the best idea is a stolen one. Why would you always try and invent something new when someone may already have a good idea that worked. At the Conventions it was also in the hospitality suites that we booked the majority of the entertainment over some beers. It was the easiest way to route the entertainers, wherever they may be from. Agents presented everything from bands and thrill shows to walk-about entertainers and monster truck shows. You name it, it was likely available at this time. These nights had all of the buyers and players in the same room. All of the agents were there and we could discuss options and budgets with our colleagues and get the deal done, then have another beer. This is where I learned to deal with Agents.

We were pretty happy winning the award for sure as it was the start of a big turnaround for this Exhibition. I didn't gloat as we went past the Brandon table at the awards banquet, as I learned a lot there, but I must admit I felt vindicated and knew I was in fact ready for the job. I just had to make the decision to be more mature and be prepared to move for the next opportunity. Making a change was on me.

I'll always remember at that same convention I was attending one of the various seminars and they had a speaker telling us how we had to improve our events, even though he hadn't actually been at any type of a fair for over eight years. I had asked some questions and politely called out some of his suggestions and he actually told me, "Well, that's why you have a bad fair."

So tell me when I was up on the stage getting our award in front of the majority of the Canadian Fair Industry that I didn't want to start my acceptance speech with "Hey buddy, how's my bad fair now, go fuck yourself." Amazingly I didn't and when we got back to Yorkton we had a great party with the remainder of the Directors and Volunteers. It was a real positive turning point for the organization.

Back again at one of our events we had another trip and fall, which was common for sure. This time it was an older lady who had stepped wrong off the curb, fell down and broke her leg. Well her older Ukrainian husband was now in the office, not bitching to us about the injury, but instead he wanted to know who was now going to cook for him. And this was why I loved my first boss there as President. He turned and said, "What, did she break her arm too?" That went over like a lead balloon, but later I laughed my ass off. What a perfect response, and we didn't hear back from him.

When I was in this business I had to do some crazy shit for promotion. Bungee jumping and things like that were easy, but try singing on the Grandstand with a live band in front of about 3,000 people. Check.

I spoke with one of the local promotion managers of a radio station saying that I wanted to do something different as a promotion to which he agreed. We tried to come up with something that may get noticed. I then made a bet with him that I could beat him in a goat milking contest, with the loser having to go on stage and sing at the very popular Star Search Competition. Well this may have been a good idea at the time, until I was getting closer to the actual event, and the fact I had never milked anything in my life, well almost anything, and I was getting nervous. Of course he didn't want to sing on the stage either. So we agreed we would both sing, but I had to get us disqualified so we would both lose. Well I did beat him in the contest, though milking a goat was never on a bucket list for sure, but after I won, I went and kicked over his pail and off to the Grandstand it was. My kids were there knowing I would be up on Stage and wanted to hide. Geez no eye for talent I suppose. I ensured I had some rum courage before; we changed the words of a country song, the Watermelon Crawl, to make it more local, the Exhibition Crawl, we sang with the band, and even got a standing ovation. I'll also guarantee my singing career ended there. We laughed our asses off. Wasn't army singing for sure, and I didn't have to throw anyone on the ground after.

I also ate Prairie Oysters in this business as well. If you don't know what those are, look it up. Even army rations weren't as disgusting as that.

This was an industry where you really had to adapt to the environment, in a sense, kind of like being in the field. We were very much a weather oriented business, especially during Summer Fairs, because over that amount of days we were almost guaranteed ugly weather somewhere. If a storm happened, which always seemed to happen, the crowd was running indoors while we were running out.

As Managers we really had to know something about everything. Contracts, agriculture, horses, rodeo, chuck wagons, carnies, 4-H, entertainment, sponsorship, budgets, negotiations, community relations, midways, scheduling, media and a few dozen other things. This was a great job for thinking on your feet, especially problem solving. It was the old, would you rather know 100% of 1 thing or 1% of a 100 things. The industry was also very good at sharing experiences and resources, no matter if it was the Calgary Stampede or mid-sized fairs like the one I was at. Really was good Canadian Teamwork.

Maybe our politicians could take a lesson from Exhibitions on how to nation build instead of always trying to divide us. Seemed they always showed up at our events wanting to say how great we were, then say something different out of the public eye. I remember one Mayor, after saying nice things in public, advocating for us to be moved out of the offices we were in because he didn't like the contract that was negotiated before his time. Another example was the Summer Fair Parade. I mean to most people a Parade is a Parade however the Parade was the event which brought the most people into town in one day throughout the entire year. There were thousands of people from around the area. So what did our City reward us with? They decided the day before the parade that they would oil the streets of entire parade route. Of course there was outrage, especially from us, and the only thing that kind of saved them was there was a massive downpour the night before that washed most of it off. From the City, no one even had enough spine to admit who gave the order to do this. It pissed us off, but we knew just where we stood with city administration sometimes for sure. There was the usual apologies and crap, but to us they were hollow and it was too late.

I got involved with the Board for Saskatchewan Fairs called SAASE (Saskatchewan Association of Agricultural Societies and Exhibitions). Try fitting that handle on a hockey jersey. I was eventually elected to the Board and later became President. As an organization we dealt very closely with all of the Fairs around the province. There were around seventy to eighty, if I remember right, from small hamlet towns to the cities. Exhibitions are certainly about history, and many of them were around before towns were even developed. So they were among the builders of many cities and towns in the late 1800's and early 1900's. I was involved in many meetings with government officials, other than photo ops, but they also provided grant money to many of the organizations. I also created a province wide marketing campaign that was a lot of work but very rewarding. Developed a strategy to market all of our Fairs and Exhibitions in the Province, wrote the commercials for TV and voiced them all as well. I also did all of the commercial writing, or most of it anyway, for the Exhibition when I was the Manager. I just wanted our commercials to sound different than the many on the air. It helped that I have a warped sense of humor, well that's what Rui always told me.

Things were going pretty well in those days. I left though for a couple of reasons. First, the guy running our local Mall was leaving and he told me I should apply for his job. I hadn't the first damn clue what he did, so he laid it all out for me and it sounded interesting enough. It was also, for the most part, was an actual day job. At this point in my life I didn't know what a regular day job was. The other reason was, while the first two Presidents I worked for were good men then next one coming was someone I didn't trust. There is no doubt we would have bumped heads pretty hard. I had called him out a couple times when he was lying. I didn't need that grief anymore, no matter how good I was at the job.

Part of it though was in this business, much like the media, if you wanted the bigger coin you'd have to move to bigger Fairs. I had two young kids by then and I just didn't want to do the moving around anymore. Though my kids sure loved it when I was running the Fair, free tickets, and they could go pretty much when they wanted, especially for the Summer Fair.

Life goes way too fast for us though as I went from helping them on the Kiddie Rides to now meeting them in the Beer Gardens. They got the chance to grow up in Yorkton and didn't have to move around, which I know in the end they appreciated. Once they grew up I took the opportunity to move.

This Was The Sanity Location For 25-years Each May Long In Duck Mountain, Manitoba And Bonus....Phone Didn't Work There

So not long after I applied at the Mall, was interviewed, and after a few months I was offered the job. It was also the first time I negotiated my salary, as they were offering the same as what I was making in the Fair Business. I held my ground and said, "What the hell would I do that for when I was already well regarded in the Fair Industry." I also wanted some security, as I knew the Mall was for sale and didn't want to get over there, find out it sold, and then the new owners would immediately turf me, which happens way too often. Long story short, I got the job, the funds I asked for, and was finally making more than the army days. Well geez that didn't take long, only about twelve years.

"You're not going to make it on Civvy Street Okrainec."

I also negotiated that if the Mall sold within the first twelve months I was employed and if I was let go for any reason by the new ownership group that they would pay me out a year's wages. To my surprise they agreed. They must have been hard up with not many people wanting to move to the booming metropolis of Yorkton. As it turned out it was a damn good thing I negotiated that clause as three months later the Mall sold, and it was an ugly turnover, which I'll get to later.

Knowing it would take some time for the Board to find my replacement at the Exhibition I did the nice thing and gave six weeks' notice to help them out. I was then surprised that they took away all of my signing authority and kept me in the dark for the final weeks like somehow it was now the secret service. It was completely unnecessary and I was pretty disappointed. I guess they had their reasons, but it's not like this was some major corporation. It made for a very long six weeks.

I did have a fun farewell **in** the end. With the Ag guys the go to drink in the barns was Sambuca, which could be found in many a TAC box for sure. So one of the presents I received was three bottles of Sambuca and through the night I had a shot with each director. Not a full shot as that stuff is nasty. Ugghhh. It did hurt the next day. Like I said I was proud of the fact leaving and they were debt free. They were the organization who gave me a chance and I wished them well.

They sure struggled for the next couple of years though with Managers coming in with no experience. Near the end of my time with them, when things were rolling, there were those who were taking credit for things they had nothing to do with but where nowhere to be found when things went wrong and were prepared to point the finger in my direction. That was sometimes the downside of volunteer boards.

I remember sitting around at one of our events near the end of the day having a beer in one of our bars and Lee Odelein, Lyle's brother from the NHL, who was the coach of the SJHL Terriers, came by. He was a good guy and sat down at our table. It was also a time when the team wasn't doing very well. When his team was doing well his board was taking a lot of the credit, but now they were struggling it was on him and he was taking some heat. As all coaches do. So he sits down and I start bugging him about the team and it was his entire fault. His buddy told me he had to drag him over as he didn't want to sit down as everyone was saying the same thing. Then, when he sits down, the first fuckin thing I do is start giving him the gears. I turned to Lee and said, "Hey man, I live your life every day the same way." He chuckled and we got along just fine. The couple of Directors sitting with me were none too pleased, but truth hurts sometimes I guess.

When I did leave and they finally hired someone to replace me I offered help and to call me if the new Manager had any questions. I respected the organization but it was quite obvious the new Manager wasn't ready for the position and really had no management experience at all. It was a rough go.

Now if you offer help you follow through, but after three or four months of receiving five phone calls a week I finally blew a stack and chewed her out as I was trying to learn my new job. She was also blaming me for things going wrong over there to the board and I was pissed and told her off. We were also a major sponsor so she wasn't expecting it.

While I do not gloat, I did feel vindicated later when a Director told me they didn't know what they had until I was gone. To me change happens everywhere. I wasn't the first to come and go.

My last booking in that industry was Kenny Shields and Streetheart, as they were one of my favorite bands, and I had got to know Kenny over the years. I heard sadly he passed away not long ago. I was already at the Mall when the next Summer Fair rolled around and had him come and do an autograph session at the Mall before he played the concert at the Fair, and of course I went to the show that night. There were some people annoyed though as during the concert he thanked me and not the Exhibition, like I had anything to do with that.

For me, the Exhibition has been around for over 120-years and they certainly would survive with or without me. I would never wish them ill will for sure. There were some really great people there.

So now it was off to the corporate world of Property Management. Where the companies are located across the entire country and at times staff seem like just a number and where Corporate seems only concerned about money, their shareholders and profits. This was more fact in the early part of my career. Not so much now. It can be a tough world to work in, especially if you are not used to it. All I could do was try and focus on the region I worked and hope there was a boss willing to go to bat for us when the time came.

And into this world steps Richard Ernie "Go Fuck Yourself" Okrainec. Well this should go very well. I mean what could go wrong!! It was also my first ever basically 9-5 job. Having my evenings free for the first time was very different for sure. I had to get a life.

I started this adventure in 1999. Basically, in this job you essentially are the Landlord of all the retail spaces, deal in very large numbers, as far as rent and operations, and enforce the terms of the lease agreement. It is also important to know the agreements inside and out. There is normally a Head Office in Toronto or Calgary and when in a place like I was, we were very much on our own for the most part. People rarely came to visit the Centre. This would mean they would have to go off the beaten path from what they were used to from the larger cities. This was more prevalent if the only office was in the east and they knew nothing of the small city west. Even more true if the property is located in nowhere Saskatchewan, well nowhere in their minds. 95% of the time it was good for that reason, but the 5% they were needed they weren't around and it could be tough. I learned to live with it.

So knowing I was going to work at the Mall and I wouldn't get a holiday for a while I went to see my good buddy Boyd just outside of Edmonton for the weekend prior to starting. So after a weekend of storytelling and drinking I was ready to head back on the Sunday for my first day on Monday. And wouldn't you know it I got fogged in for the day and couldn't make it to my first day of work as there were no flights until Monday. Well just fucking great. So on the first day of the job I had to phone the staff to tell them I wouldn't be in and of course the first thought is I slept in. I never sleep in, but ya terrific start to this career. Likely in trouble right off the hop if I still had a job.

So the world I was moving on to was interesting for sure. I got there Tuesday and my boss was based out of Regina at the time. Well he didn't even call to check on me for two weeks and didn't even know I missed my first day until I told him. Ya he really cared about us. Not. I knew then we were on our own.

And sure a shit, three months later the Mall was sold, and I was welcomed officially to the corporate world. I didn't hear from the new Management Group for over a month or from the owners for about three months.

I eventually did get a call from someone who said they were my boss. She talked to me for five minutes then sent me my one year evaluation noting that I was below standard and that all staff would be starting with no seniority

Naturally I took that well.

"You know where you can put that evaluation, I'm certainly not going to sign it and please don't call back until I have a chance to speak with the staff and the Labour Board." I mean really WTF.

The seniority reduction never happened and I didn't sign the evaluation.

So after about three months of trying to keep things together, not knowing who to answer to or just who to call, I start thinking, "Where's my field pay?"

So out of the blue we get this call while I was in the front office.

I say, "Hi, Richard here."

To which the reply was, "What the fuck is going on at that place, it's one big clusterfuck."

"Just a second I need to go to my office and talk from there."

Pissed off and back in my office I pick up the phone to see if he is still there. I then reply,

"Who the fuck is this? Don't be calling and asking what the fuck is going on when I haven't the first clue who you are. You left me hanging here for over three months. Just say hi."

Turns out he was the VP of Operations and was an F...Bomber as well. We ended up getting along just fine.

HR did call the next day from the Management Group and said it likely isn't a good idea telling off the VP. Ya whatever.

Receiving My Peace Keeping Medal In My Home Town Legion

Usually my issues almost always ended up being with the Leasing crew. They are the ones who negotiate the Leases. We all had to live with the promises they made which we'd have to keep, from which these promises wouldn't be known until a copy of the agreement was received. As with anything there were many good ones over the years. It was the few who grated on me that made me frustrated. This was more prevalent in the early part of my career.

Back then they also didn't last very long either. I had a run of eight Leasing people in eight years. They sure came and went.

Tenants who didn't have much experience with Leases wouldn't know what they had to actually pay until we prepared their payment schedule and many times they wouldn't be happy campers. Then the Leasing person was gone and we'd have to deal with it and live with the promises we had nothing to do with. Always fun.

Also at times they wouldn't put directions or orders in writing when required. I used to give them grief at times and wouldn't do a task because they wouldn't put it in writing. You had to cover your ass in this business.

I had one, who was one of those who never would take responsibility for mistakes and certainly was not someone I even remotely trusted. He messed up a deal, I mean he's the one who does them, but tried to lay if on me. Geez where has that happened to me before? He was even at my office telling my staff he didn't blame them but blamed me.

After finding out this had happened he was later in my office and blamed me. So naturally I said, "You know you can go fuck yourself."

He didn't take kindly to this but didn't realize just how much I wanted to shit kick him. It didn't matter though as the staff knew who buggered the deal. Not long after my boss was down and I told her the story. She asked if I really said that. I said, "Yes," and prepared for whatever. In the end she was cool with it and it was never mentioned on my evaluation.

Not long after same guy phoned me at home on a Sunday morning as his deal went south with dollars involved. I let him know I was eating breakfast and would call him back, but he kept on bitching to me, so I just hung up on him. I then sent an e-mail to my boss telling the story while also being prepared to drive to where he lived and shit kick him. She ended up talking me down and took care of things.

Now-a-days when leaving a corporate job, or many jobs where there is a head office, they are big on exit interviews. I'm not sure if they really cared but they wanted to do one none the less.

Well over my years in this industry there was a time I got a new boss and there really is no polite words to describe her. Easily, in my life, the worst boss I ever had, and that's saying something. It was to a point I was going home pissed off most days and needed to go sit by myself for an hour so not to take it out on the family.

It was all good timing when I did get a call from a head hunter about another position with a different company and having the opportunity to get the hell out. She ruined some of the careers of my colleagues. I did hear there finally was some karma though, as she was marched out later. I was so sad, but it was too late for some of my friends who she burned.

So on the last day when I was leaving and after having a farewell with the staff, with my office all packed up and keys returned she called near the end of the day, not to say goodbye, but for me to get a report done right damn now. The Property Administrator took the call and I refused to speak with her and I heard her barking that I better take the call, but I just left. In all my years I don't think I've had the displeasure of working with someone like that.

So HR called wanting to do this exit interview. I asked if they wanted to be patronized or wanted the truth. She noted they always want the truth. Well I was leaving anyway so I gave them the truth, the army version.

The interview was just a bunch of standard questions until she got to the part about what I thought of the leadership I worked for.

I replied, "Ok, I`ll answer it this way. Please keep in mind that I am going to use army terminology and will mention guns and bullets, but this is just an example and not to be taken literally."

She said, "That is more than fine. We encourage honesty."

"When I was in the army and became a leader I tried to look after the troops and at the very least be fair. I didn't continually screw them over and go on power trips. That was because I knew eventually I may have to go to battle with them. What I did not want was to be on the attack and the ramp of the track is going down and I was out front leading the advance only to be shot in the back by my own troops."

"So by that example and back with this company, we are now advancing and she is leading, the ramp goes down and she's leading the attack.......bang. That's my thoughts on the leadership."

There was a long pause before she thanked me for my time and that was the last I heard from the HR. Sometimes you lose and sometimes you get field pay.

I Really Was A City Councillor

I started paying attention to City Politics when I ran the largest building in the City. It was also along that route I became the Chamber President. I also liked Municipal Politics because we all lived in the same town and issues were dealt with. I also learned not tick off seniors because most of them vote. I don't remember what the issues of the day were but like many around the City

I wasn't happy with what was going on. So instead of whining I put my name on the ballot. The problem was so did seventeen others for six spots. I finished seventh, but did learn a lot and I ran again the next time and got elected.

I remember thinking there was a good chance I was getting elected so I told my boss. She wasn't impressed, but I let her know I read the employee handbook and it specifically noted I didn't have to tell my employer if I was running for Municipal Council. Once I was officially elected she gritted her teeth and congratulated me.

She was more worried about confidential information being disclosed by me when it may not benefit them, but then wanted to know things from the City from which I wouldn't tell her. Confidentiality in reverse if the benefit was only one way. What a circus.

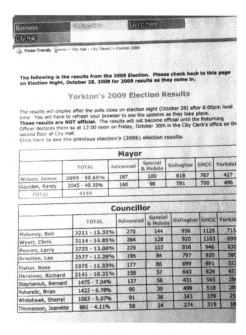

Municipal Election Results

I survived it all and did one term, though it did make for a very busy life while also running three properties, including two in Winnipeg. I was a bit disappointed when I didn't get re-elected, but in the end I didn't stay one term too long like many of them and later saw everyone but one was voted out the last election. Such is local politics. It probably didn't help that I wasn't always political for sure. Like I said, at least in Municipal Politics no one gets away with anything and issues get resolved for the most part. It seems helpless getting issues resolved Provincially or Federally.

The Leasing crew in the early days were quite difficult to deal with, as I mentioned, and some tried to treat me like some hick town manager. It was really painful for them to come to my centres, especially in Saskatchewan. We didn't have a passenger airport so they had to fly to Regina and then drive a couple hours to where we were. Yorkton is a smaller agricultural city and doesn't have $300 Hiltons, so they never stayed overnight. Having an expense account at your disposal made you fussier.

One day, I'll say he was John A. Smith. On his way from Regina he got pulled over by the police about halfway to Yorkton. It turned out there was a Canada wide warrant for John B. Smith who was wanted for murder and he was dragged out of the car and was spread eagle on the hood and searched, until they found out they had the wrong guy. "Have a nice day." He came and then never came back for some reason. I laughed my ass off.

I had another who came down in the winter and we ended up getting a pretty bad blizzard and roads were getting closed. Our hotels didn't have enough class for him so he hit the road for Regina. He got about halfway, in the same area as the story above, only to find out the roads were closed. He was then forced to stay in a two star motel for the night. I laughed my ass off and he never came back again either. It was like field pay.

Still another different one came down who really was an arrogant guy. He brought down a client with him and was trying to be the big shot and talking down to me, which usually doesn't go over very well. As with the time of year we had a lot of gravel on the streets and he was bitching to me that the city should clean the streets.

I just said, "They don't have rocks in Calgary."

He said, "It's pretty pathetic and let's hope it's better for the next time I come."

I told him to hold that thought and pretended to call the City Manager, who I knew well, and said,

"Hi, ya it's Richard over at the Mall. I have a leasing guy here from Calgary who isn't very happy with all the gravel on the streets and wants it cleaned up......No, I know we just finished winter and why there is so much, apparently they don't make gravel in Calgary.....He says ya we'll get right on that.....not."

He was pretty pissed but his client thought it was funny. He was fired not long after and I never saw him again.

Dealing in the corporate world can be very interesting, especially those who were born and bred in the large cities and who know nothing about the small town west. So when making a speech one day at a Chamber Business Awards Banquet I gave everyone a fictional story that wasn't far off reality. Like the Recruiter.

The story was when I was at the Mall telling a few sales people how important I was with the company and the Corporation completely respected me and even though I am here they know who I am, when suddenly my phone rang. I looked down and seen it was our HR Department. I said,

"See I told you I'm important," and answered the phone.

"Hello,"

"Yes hello, is Richard Organdufus there?"

Sigh..."Ya that's me."

Yes Mr. Okraindork. I just wanted to let you know we got your application for one of the positions here at the Corporate Office. I must say, the Board of Directors near soiled themselves when they saw your qualifications. So, good luck in Sasktewatchin."

I replied, "Hey, it's Saskatchewan and we have the hottest economy in the country right now."

She laughed and said, "Ha Saskewatchin, we get more people at a Leafs Game than you have out there."

So now I am annoyed and say, "You know, there is no difference between our pro hockey team out here and your Leafs."

She replied, "What, you don't have a pro hockey team out there."

I said, "Exactly!" and quickly hung up the phone.

I didn't get the position.

Doing My Time As Chamber President

Occasionally I still did fun dumb shit as well. One day I attended the Lyle Odelein Charity Golf Tourney and it turned into a shit show. There were lots of hammered people there. So now it was after supper and I, like many others, was quite liquored and said to a buddy from the Mall, "Let's go for a ride." He got on the golf cart with his beer and we headed out. So now after we go over the exit speed bump he asked, "Just where the fuck we were going." I said, "To Burger King." Well we were about five miles from town it was dark and headed out. Just like blackout driving back in those Army Days. The trip at top speed took about two hours and in all that time we didn't see a car on the gravel road into town or the streets in town. We did crash once however as we were cruising down one of the streets, I dropped my smoke, bent down to pick it up and the wheel turned and we crashed into someone's front yard and I fell off and cracked my kneecap. Dumbfuck. This was no army roll or Bruce Lee landing. It was just......splat. Much like the duck I took out I suppose. We laughed got back on and made it to the Superstore Parking lot, and Burger King was on the other side. Well after finally seeing our end goal of food, I then noticed a truck was following me and I tried to lose him around the gas pumps, in a golf cart, and he pulled up and said, "Okrainec, what the fuck are you doing?" He was the Manager of the Golf Course. I chucked him the keys and ran into the Boston Pizza Lounge.

Well I called him the next day, once I sobered up, with a cracked kneecap, and offered to pay for any damage. He said there wasn't any, but let me know just after I got into BP's the cops showed up, as they were called by Citizens on Patrol. It must have been the yard crash, go figure. They were pissed off and asked who was driving and he told them he didn't know and that he just found the cart in the lot. They laughed and loaded the cart and took it back to the course. Like field pay.

What a night. I didn't walk straight for about 6-months though.... Dumbfuck. It would just add to the legends of stories out there. He told me of one of our Exhibition Directors, who used to work out there, was really hammered one night and the police found him in a golf cart two or three miles from the course crashed in the ditch at 2:00 in the morning. They knew him and yelled to him,

"Glen, what the fuck are you doing?"

From which Glen replied, "What the fuck do you think I'm doing, I'm looking for my ball."

They laughed their asses off and gave him a ride home.

Once I was in the industry long enough I had the opportunity to chase money to move up the ladder, but I really wasn't interested. I was now used to not moving around and I also knew I wouldn't survive in a Corporate Office very long without speaking my mind or hurting someone. Being in out of the way Malls suited me just fine. I had more head office visitors in Winnipeg when I travelled there for sure.

Over the years I also took the difficult and in depth Real Estate Course. This was over a year long journey to complete when I had time. It included Property Management, Real Estate Law, Finance and Basic Real Estate. You never stop learning.

I also got in the habit from the media days to record things, just in case, plus I could always listen back to ensure I understood whatever instructions I was to move forward with. I did this more so I wouldn't miss something and always erase the info when done. This was always a good way to ensure I wouldn't take anything out of context. I used this mostly for Conference Calls or Interviews just to keep my notes together. If I was recording someone I had to let the person know. I have many times over the years had people ask me to do something I deemed questionable, so I would let them know I was now recording the conversation and would ask them to repeat what they said, for the record, or to put the request in writing. Some would not repeat or put in writing and tell me to do it anyway and I would just refuse. I would just say, "Hold on can you say that again while I am recording," then there would be a pissed of click of the phone hanging up. I knew who I had to watch out for.

As for staff, really from day one, I tried to treat them fair with the only request to do their job. Over the years, like any manager, I had to let some people go, but no matter how much they deserved it, it was never easy. Though I imagine when that happened they could care less how I felt. I tried to let the departments run themselves and not micro manage and I think they appreciated it. Someone shouldn't be afraid to make mistakes, unless it's a pretty big money mistake, which happened, and I had to let someone go as a result. I've had claims laid against me for wrongful dismissal but in this world the issue is handled by HR and not the site. Not fun to go through though. I find it much harder watching them bash me on social media and I'm not allowed to reply in case it buggers up the claim. Everything in this world is a liability world.

Still had interesting dealings with some staff over the years though.

One time I had one come in with a labor standards book and let me know some of the things I was doing wrong, according to the book. I said, "Fair enough. Tomorrow I'll put in a punch clock for all staff. At coffee I'll hang down and the Food Court to ensure coffee is only fifteen minutes and not the usual forty five which was going on now. We'll likely need to put together a daily work progress report or you can put the book away and go to work.'

He went to work.

Had another note he wasn't happy with his wage and didn't feel like he was making the industry standard, whatever that was.

I said, "Fair enough, just let me know when you are leaving for the standard." He didn't leave.

One had broken up with the girlfriend and wanted a raise because he couldn't afford being single. I mean what do you do with that, other than why does the company have to pay for the break up?

One thing that became very useful for me was when I got really ticked off was I would go for a walk through the Mall. Though certainly some days I had to cruise a lot more than others, especially with the one boss I had a while back. But I needed that walk before replying to an e-mail as an e-mail is forever.

I've also, over time, tried to hire military brothers when I had an opportunity. Two of them were hired as staff where I worked, and the other was signed to a contract. One was a hard worker, but just couldn't keep his mouth shut and always was in trouble or telling someone off. He just didn't do himself favors, but it was the way he was. The other with the contract ended badly as he didn't fulfill his obligations and just never came back. I knew however he was having issues from one of the tours so I just let it go. And the last one was still around and in fact had now been in the position longer than I was with the company. It turned into a second career.

I had mentioned I was given the Strip Mall in Winnipeg and travelled there from Yorkton every five or six weeks initially. It was a five hour trip. I needed someone I could trust to work unsupervised as there was no office in Winnipeg or another Property in the area the company managed. So I tracked down my buddy Clay Rankin, worked on him for a while and he finally decided to come over and be in charge of Maintenance/Operations. He's been a close buddy for many years, and was also later part of the fishing crew each May long. I knew he was someone I could trust who would show up every day. I let my boss know that we knew each other and she agreed with my logic to hire him. That's when I found out his name was Robert and he found out my name was Richard. After almost 40-years we found out our first names. Go figure.

Poor old Clay paid for it though some days, when I was putting up with my difficult boss and had no one to take it out on. Then I would look at the call display and see it was Clay. I'd chew him out for nothing he'd give it back and ask what I was pissed off about, then we would go play a round of golf and he would forgive me. My only round ever in the 70's was with Robert or whatever his name is. He shot in the 70's as well. What was that score Clayton??? Oh ya I painted it on your wall at work. After all these years he has since covered the score over. I don't speak about how he almost always beat me at every other round we played. That's different you know! And also, he may have usually beat me, but I have a Hole in One. I remember that day not long ago, being pumped that I got a Hole in One, rushed home to tell my wife from which she replied, "What's a hole in one?" Well that sucked the life out of my joy, until I could brag to someone else.

With staff I have had to deal with some pretty scary things as well. After a time I was also given control of a large enclosed Centre in Winnipeg, plus the Strip Clay was working at, and the one in Yorkton. I ended up with more staff in Winnipeg and sometimes had to travel twice a month. The travel was really getting old after ten years. During that time I've had a couple staff almost die, some others with very serious illnesses and through it all I tried to ensure no matter where I was, that they would be taken care of. Even if I was in El Salvador, which happened to me as well, well not to me but to the staff member of course. Did what I could from far away until I returned to Canada.

As I am getting to the end of my career I feel it's my job to pass the information and experience down and what they do with it is up to them. Life is about experiences and how we deal with situations, no matter what they are. If I had dealt with something in the past I pass on how I dealt with it, and hope it helps someone get through a situation. Likely one of the hardest aspects I had to deal with when becoming a Senior Member of the Team is all the generations that worked for me and trying to balance each one. Christ man. It wasn't that way in the army was it? Maybe, but most of us grew up together and also were posted at a base for a while, so it seemed different.

I have hired younger staff just to get a succession plan in place as when I looked around I saw many of the Managers were the same age as me or older. I just had a meeting with them prior to the hiring and said pass the knowledge as there likely will be hiccups along the way, but we all started somewhere. They were good about it.

I learned as well in this business that the customer isn't always right, not even close. I had one f-bombing me because the height restrictor at the Mall took out his AC unit on his Motorhome. Well that's why we had height restrictors. He told me he didn't know how high his AC unit was and that he was sick of these hick town malls. Of course he didn't like it when I noted that he likely now knew that it's higher than the sign where the height restrictor was, and where he wasn't supposed to be driving. He started f-bombing me again and was being a prick in general and after a while I noted if he kept f-bombing me I was going to teach him how to fly as we were on the 2nd floor.

There was another guy who called and told me I was a prick because I wouldn't give him equipment that was left as part of a Tenant abandoning. I asked him to come to the mall to say that to my face, which of course he didn't. My boss kind of freaked about that. I just said I certainly didn't need them pussy footing around and never defending me, by doing nothing. Now-a-days when customers don't get their way, even if they are wrong, they just take to social media and you just have to ride out the storm and not keep it alive, as my one boss notes. Good advice most of the time. I just try not to read the comment boards, otherwise I would be even more grey and pissed off. I always find it amazing how many people know what's going on in some situation or are telling people how they should have dealt with it. Even when they do not have the first clue about what really happened and were not there when it happened. The brave keyboard warriors.

I can't believe that I will soon be rolling into twenty years in the Corporate World, with only a limited amount of "Go fuck yourself" along the way. It's been a journey. There have been some great people along the way. One of my bosses has a line for us to stay in our lane. Well that's what I tried to do, just sometimes I was driving with my blinker on. The one constant I had on almost all of my yearly evaluations throughout the years was "Richard is too protective of his staff". Well after what happened to me in my younger years, someone had to be. I also knew if push came to shove I would always have their back, and not worry what would happen when the ramp went down. Well, most of them anyway. To the staff along the way, it's not easy to be in charge, but thanks for being you.

It's funny I was in the army for eight plus years and have now managed to work on Civvy Street for over thirty.

"You're not going to make it on Civvy Street Okrainec." Ya whatever.

There is one thing I know. Those days with my brothers shaped me in a big way that a guy just doesn't forget or can shake. And over time I have come to realize.........

I'm just not the same anymore.

As for my brothers, well I have managed to see some of you at Beer Calls along the way. As I read the many proofs of this story it suddenly dawned on me just how many brothers, friends and colleagues I have lost from my military days. There are quite a few noted in the story. That also doesn't include the ones lost from the Bosnia and Afghanistan tours, plus having very close brothers dealing with PTSD. It really hit me, and made me very sad. I wish all their families nothing but best wishes and all the best.

Beer Call Edmonton

Beer Call Edmonton

And of course the Kapyong Tear Down get together in Winnipeg

Several Generations of the 2nd Battalion

Dennis....a brother from a different mother

Through the journey I have also had the opportunity to speak at schools, elementary and high school, the Legion, and was also the guest speaker for the Remembrance Day Ceremony one year in Yorkton. I spoke of what I thought, the experiences and some stories, like many other veterans have done and still do.

Of course there were two main questions I always got.

"How many Medals do you have?" From which I say, "Yes."

The other is, "Have you killed anyone?" with the polite reply being, "Could you? It's not a video game."

And leave it at that.

CHAPTER 9
The Wrap-up

I, for the most part, kept politics and some opinions out of my story. I kind of saved it for the final portion. It will give you an idea how my mind works, what gets me worked up and my weird sense of humor. The other points are just something to think about.

You'll get the idea when you get that far.

I likely would be considered a fiscal conservative, but I'm not sure what that means anymore as no government can spend within their means. I believe in government not running my life and that I shouldn't have to give 44% of the money back in various taxes, only to get taxed more because no government can resist spending our money. And now with the globalist movement so much money is being sent to other countries and we are not taking care of our own people. It's our damn money. It really frustrates me.

So for the next while there will be a snap chat version of what's on my mind, including where my mind wanders.

It's called: JUST HOW SHOULD I FEEL

So it's from this Dirty Patricia to you.

But first: The Dirty Patricia

You have obviously seen a few pictures in the story with the Dirty Patricia gear. The story of the Dirty Patricia is folklore or a myth and something in-between. It's been told, but never confirmed, that after the Patricia's were involved in a bloody battle from an earlier war the remaining bloody and filthy troops came down the hill and eventually were having drinks remembering their brothers who didn't make it. It is said an officer came around from a different unit and wasn't impressed the way they looked and said to another officer from the Patricia's, "Who are those filthy soldiers?" to which the officer replied, "Those are my Dirty Patricia's."

I could not confirm the story and maybe it is just a myth. I did however track down Joel "Pipes" Turnbull, who produces the gear in various fashions and he explained it more plainly. There was a comment from another infantry unit who happened to be instructing or taking the same course he was on from which he noted tongue and cheek, "That's what happens when you put a Dirty Patricia in charge." It could also be, "The Princess Pat's, doing Canada's Dirty work for over 104-years."

In the end I believe it's really much more simple than any of that, though each soldier may have their own version. It's about that dirty, filthy, tired soldier that keeps moving forward. And it's something those of us who have served in any of the facets of the military can relate to.

So to all you Dirty Patricia's and all veterans out there. This part is for you.

RICHARD (ERNIE) OKRAINEC

This Dirty Patricia has feelings

Just how should I feel

Just how should I feel when our government sends our military to a faraway land to fight terrorism and when they return the government fights them in court for benefits but pays the terrorist.

Just how should I feel that our governments have spent billions upon billions of our tax dollars to despot countries while we still have thousands of our own living in poverty or who are homeless.

Just how should I feel when you are not allowed to ask how the over $10-billion is spent on Indigenous Affairs to be provided to First Nations while still having reserves without the basics of running water or housing.

Just how should I feel that I live in a country that used to have a law where it was illegal to cut the tag off the mattress. To this day I am still waiting for the MP`s (Mattress Police) to knock on my door and say, "I have warrant to inspect your mattress."

Just how should I feel that the current government told us they paid the terrorist to save us in legal fees, yet have spent over $100,000 in legal bills fighting a dental claim of $6,000 of a First Nations child.

Just how should I feel when all governments keep telling us they are concerned about our household debt yet they keep increasing our taxes and the fact that there is not one Province or the Federal Government who are not in massive debt with no repayment plan in place.

Just how should I feel when governments keep taking away our ability to save for retirement and closing our options but they do not ever change their gold plated pension plans that the taxpayer must fund.

Just how should I feel that one night when channel surfing I came upon Wheel of Fortune and one of the contestants had a patch over his eye and I couldn't leave the room until I heard him say, "I would like to buy an I Pat."

Just how should I feel that when I lie I am called out and vilified but when a politician blatantly lies, it's called politics.

Just how should I feel when people who are actors and actresses whose job it is to pretend to be someone else, yet continue to tell me how I should be living my life when my life is not an act.

Just how should I feel then when all the sex scandals hit Hollywood, Politics & the Media to find out that many knew and covered it up or didn't speak about it until after because they wanted to start a movement. Yet they speak about rights and how other people should speak up and empower themselves. I'm sorry your fantasy world is bullshit.

Just how should I feel when musicians or famous people who die as a result of drugs or liquor are then celebrated as artists, while if you are just a regular person who is an addict and dies of the same cause you were just an addict who deserved to die.

Just how should I feel that when I was in school way back when I was taught I before E except after C. I now know this is a complete lie I am starting to doubt everything I was taught in school and those classes I failed should now be credited to me.

Just how should I feel if I have a different opinion about why the climate is changing and I am labelled as a denier, yet all Climate Conferences are held in all the 5 star resorts around the world, never in a hardship area or with poor weather, and the last one alone featured over 1,500 private jets, severely damaging the planet they so care for if their cause was completely true.

Just how should I feel that at this same conference, where Canada brought over 300 people to save the planet, we found out one bureaucrat expensed meals over $30,000 saving the planet with taxpayer funds, while if I did the same thing I would be immediately fired.

Just how should I feel when small business across the country who employ over 70% of the jobs in the nation are now labelled as tax cheats yet the two people who are spearheading tax changes are millionaires from which their sheltered funds are protected

Just how should I feel about the Kardashians. WTF is that about?

Just how should I feel that the same tax changes will not affect the big banks and all their massive service fees and multi-billion dollar profits, yet the, cough cough, middle class are being looked after.

Just how should I feel that I was raised from which if you worked hard you'll have success and with success will come more money only for the government to say, "You know what, you are making too much money and it's not fair, so we are going to take more from you and give it to someone else."

Just how should I feel that the major news networks no longer report the news but instead their political agenda from which you are not allowed to disagree or you are a racist.

Just how should I feel that when I was President of the Chamber of Commerce, and attended many business functions, and while at a luncheon I was speaking with the local Mortician and asked, "How's business?" to which he replied, "I wish it was busier." and looked like he was sizing me up.

Just how should I feel that there are those who somehow think the UN is the social conscience of the world, when it is filled with world leaders who have an atrocious record, including murdering or abusing their own people.

Just how should I feel then that our current government continues to throw millions upon millions at the UN in an appeared desperate attempt to obtain the non-voting seat on the Security Council. I served with the UN, in Cyprus, they were useless then and became worse after. Much worse.

Just how should I feel when our governments continue to enact policies to divide us as a nation, yet are getting paid to run the nation as one.

Just how should I feel when as a Canadian we are made fun of for being polite when I would rather that, than being made fun of for being obnoxious.

Just how should I feel that a government is elected to serve all of us yet focus mainly on their base to keep votes to stay in power instead of serving the nation.

Just how should I feel that the government in the province I live, Alberta, has told us in just 4-years we will be $72-billion in debt and that it is good for us, while smiling coming out of the presentation. To put that in perspective the Klein government took the debt from $28-billion to a positive balance sheet with much hardship. Just what in the hell are we going to do to get out of this mess without hardship?

Just how should I feel that the same government increased wages over 33% on small business with the minimum wage increase which has not increased employment and forced more costs on small business while no government worker likely makes minimum wage.

Just how should I feel that all three levels of government, Federal, Provincial and Municipal all continue to plead poverty and that there is a lack of funds for them, while all blaming each otherand wanting more from the taxpayers, when there is only one taxpayer.

Just how should I feel one day going through the Tim Horton's Drive Thru and the person in front of me paid for my coffee, and to return the favor I said I would pay for the person behind me, after checking my rear view mirror. I was informed there was no one behind me. I said thanks for the coffee and left.

Just how should I feel after attending the football game in Edmonton and finding out there was a terrorist attack that included a refugee who was to have been deported, who had an ISIS flag in one vehicle, ran people over, and a message came from the PM that we needed to end White Privilege.

Just how should I feel that on Canada Day our current PM said those of us here in Canada that were born here take it for granted and that he was jealous immigrants get a chance to choose to be Canadian rather than by default when I was born here and was prepared to die for my country and have never ever taken it for granted.

Just how should I feel growing up as a Ukrainian and being the butt of 70% of the jokes, How does a Ukrainian take a shower....Pees against the wind, How do you sink a Ukrainian boat....You put it in water....and we didn't cry, we gave it back. Now a days everyone is a pussy who gets offended or outraged over something, and for that comment I will likely be sued by the Manbun Manzee Wearing Hold My Latte Association.

Just how should I feel when I live in a country that always promoted free speech to now the speech is only free if it's the same narrative of the day.

Just how should I feel when I watch sports it was to be a getaway from the world and now it's about politics and I have moved on to other things instead.

Just how should I feel when in my day when you unfriended someone you drifted them in the face.

Just how should I feel living in today's world where on social media you can be as ignorant as you want anonymously like a coward, where I grew up in a world where if you couldn't say it to someone's face you kept your pie hole shut.

Just how should I feel when all governments say they will be more open and transparent until such time as a Freedom of Information Request and then they hide behind security concerns.

Just how should I feel when I seem to be on an island as to why Trump got elected, and while I am no big fan, he connected with the people left behind, as he said, and those without jobs who got tired of wealthy people telling them how good they have it and wanted someone who may actually try and help them with more than just words and empty promises.

Just how should I feel when I am at a self-serve gas station and while killing time filling up I see the "Call Attendant" button and I pushed it and asked what they wanted.

Just how should I feel when going back for a refill and seeing they changed the sign to read "Call Attendant For Assistance Only" so I pushed the button and asked for assistance in co-signing a loan for me.

Just how should I feel when I went back for my next refill that both my debit card and visa were declined.

Just how should I feel when hosting the Premier's Dinner put on by the Chamber and Premier Calvert said they couldn't afford to fix all the roads in the province because if they were joined together they would go around the entire earth, when I then reminded him that yes, but you also collect enough in various gas taxes to go around the earth eight times, you as governments are not using the funds for what it was intended and created for.

Just how should I feel when you fill up your tank and overfill by two or three cents and you are pissed off when they want payment for the exact amount, but you have never put $49.98 in the tank, gave a $50 and just waved and said keep it.

Just how should I feel for anyone who was ever posted to Germany that I have moved many many times over the years, to renting storage, donating things, chucking what used to be important in the garbage and the to walk around and realize, through it all, I still have five beer steins & mugs, another beer stein that holds eleven beers, a large glass boot and a boot shot glass and just can't say goodbye.

The Boot And Stein Were Put Through The Paces In Germany

Just how should I feel when a Finance Minister makes changes to the tax laws to attempt to find those gaming the system only for us to find out he was the one gaming the system.

Just how should I feel when I think the best TV Series ever was MASH followed by Breaking Bad and that the best comedy was Cheers and followed by the oldie Get Smart.

Just how should I feel when the Pope says no one should build a wall to keep people out when Vatican City is surrounded by a wall.

Just how should I feel when a wingnut from North Korea is firing missiles over Japan and is treated like the victim while Trump is being accused of trying to start WWIII. It's called treaties and you are supposed to help you allies.

Just how should I feel now that I said treaties should be honored First Nations all yelled at me "Damn Right".

Just how should I feel when I am a hard core Winnipeg Blue Bomber fan and they haven't won the Grey Cup since 1990 in an eight to nine team league.

Just how should I feel when knowing that the Blue Bombers STILL have seven more Grey Cups than the Riders. Oh nice stadium though, but you even lost the loudest stadium competition as well. Even the moose that delayed the fans couldn't help you.

Just how should I feel reading a message on Facebook where someone blamed Trump for the Hurricanes hitting Democratic areas and for people to start waking up. I mean c'mon people. And Obama didn't cause all the problems in the world either.

Just how should I feel when I go to a country I have to obey their laws but with our massive immigration taking place we are supposed to change our laws to benefit them. What the hell is that about?

Just how should I feel when I found out Drunken Canoeing was removed from the criminal code in Canada and I feel I wasted my life just canoeing sober all these years.

Just how should I feel that like most veterans I still, after 30-years, have an Ammo Can kicking around in the garage holding other stuff I'll never get rid of.

An Ammo Can Is Part Of Veteran Decor

CHAPTER 10
Conclusion of it all

So, just how do I feel. I feel great

    I married an awesome woman who keeps me grounded. From all our trials and tests we managed to raise five kids through the teenage years and integrated the families the best we could. We all survived it and are proud of what they have become in their lives. Though I must say I used to get away with a lot more when Donia didn't know English. Donia and her kids are from El Salvador. They went through the system properly, which I believe most Canadians agree it should be, learned to read and write the language and also became Canadians. When we met she spoke and understood just over 50% and I got away with a lot. Well I am proud to say those days are over and now I don't get away with anything.

My wife Donia

We married and managed to raise the kids, who are no longer kids, and are now settled into careers. While living through it and still having some hair left. And when they were teenagers I spent most nights with one eye open thinking, "Please don't be like I was."

Left to Right: Edgar, Samantha, Dirty Patricia, Donia, Stephania, Victoria and Matthew

About a decade ago we went on a trip to Mexico and saw resorts and housing on the ocean and said, "Why not us?" I mean whenever I've been down south people always talk of wanting a place. We came back to Canada and said, "Well, why can't we?" We started looking for land in El Salvador, for obvious family ties, but also that it wasn't like Mexico and we could own the land with a title. I had also been to El Salvador many times and liked the country, never having had issues. We wanted a place not to close to the family and right on the ocean.

So we made a plan of what we wanted as a place, searched a long time and eventually bought land in El Salvador which looked like this;

The original land

And turned it into this;

Out the front to the ocean

Of course with a pool bar

Not complete without a hammock area

And you never miss a sunset

Our neighbours and partners down there with a place of their own are former military colleagues and friends, Fred and Donna Hayne.

Hey, always trust a brother (and sister) and having remained good friends with them both after all these years.

Each place has 4-bedrooms with a shower, bathroom and AC in each room, because it's friggen hot there, kitchen, all the comforts of home or better. Hammock areas are to die for if you need an unconscious nap from too much tequila.

And, if any brothers need a place to get away to collect their thoughts you just need to call. If we still have the place we can work something out for you to get away from it all.

As for me. Well we are trying to get by and I'm still wiggling my toes

I hope you enjoyed what's in and now out of my head. If you didn't well, "Go fuck yourself" (lol)

I have to give a very big thanks to those who gave opinions for the journey in putting this book together. There have been several versions and drafts reviewed by many people with regards to this this project. I greatly appreciated all of your thoughts and opinions. Also a special thanks as well to my good friend and brother Clay Rankin, who not only wrote the forward, but he is also a walking thesaurus of help and suggestions which helped improve the content. As well to Bill Brown and Carlos Gomes, your input was put to use. Of course as well my mother who has read almost every version. To all, I certainly took the suggestions to heart and implemented many of them. I can't thank you enough.

And a special note to my wife Donia as well. I am sure over this journey she was tired of hearing about this project, but was patient throughout it all and gave some good advice as well. Plus the fact I won't have excuses for not doing my chores any more around the house.

I had also noted earlier about not having pictures for some of the events described in the journey, so it makes sense to also send a shout out to the various Military Facebook Groups that I am in, as in some instances a borrowed a picture or two.

To my brothers, keep being you and good luck as you find your way like I tried to do. Love every damn one of you, though seeing some of your pictures on Facebook, some of you turned out pretty ugly.

You're the best and helped me become what I am. It's because of you I'm not the same anymore....and really, I have no issues with that.

Take care

Richard (Ernie) Okrainec
VP

CPSIA information can be obtained
at www.ICGtesting.com
Printed in the USA
LVHW010116011218
598074LV00007B/24/P